D0550946

Gerhard Durlacher was born in Baden-Baden, Germany, in 1928. As a child he fled with his family to Holland, from where he was taken to a concentration camp. After the war he returned to Holland, where he taught sociology at the University of Amsterdam for many years. In his first book, *Stripes in the Sky*, Gerhard Durlacher reflected on the genocide to which he was a reluctant witness. In *Drowning*, he takes us back to his childhood, from the time he was four years old, to Hitler's rise to power and his family's flight to Holland. *The Search* carries us to various parts of the globe, as he sets off to track down a group of survivors and chronicle the stories of their lives before, during, and after the war.

Also by Gerhard Durlacher and published by
Serpent's Tail

Stripes in the Sky
Drowning

THE SEARCH

GERHARD DURLACHER

Translated by Susan Massotty

Hertfordshire Libraries,
Arts and Information

H50 362 537 6

Dic   4198

940.53 '18   £8-99

Library of Congress Catalog Card Number: 98-86405

A complete catalogue record for this book can be obtained from the British Library
on request.

The right of Gerhard Durlacher and Susan Massotty as respectively author and
translator of this work has been
asserted by them in accordance with the Copyright, Designs and Patents Act 1988.

First published as *Zoektocht* in 1991 by
Meulenhoff Nederland BV, Amsterdam

Copyright © 1991 by G. L. Durlacher and
Meulenhoff Nederland BV, Amsterdam

Translation copyright © 1998 by Susan Massotty

This edition first published in 1998 by
Serpent's Tail, 4 Blackstock Mews, London N4
Website: www.serpentstail.com

The publishers would like to acknowledge the financial support of
the Foundation for the Production and Translation of Dutch
Literature, which has made this English edition possible.

Printed in Great Britain by Mackays of Chatham, plc
Phototypeset in 10/14 pt Garamond Book by Intype London Ltd

10 9 8 7 6 5 4 3 2 1

CONTENTS

THE SEARCH

Directly in front of me on the moving walkway was a Hasidic Jew. His collar and lapels were hidden under a black beard streaked with gray. Sidelocks curled out from under a broad-brimmed black hat. A black gabardine suit was stretched tautly over his athletic shoulders.

When I tried to pass him, I noticed that his face was flushed. Piercing eyes gleamed terrifyingly behind a pair of thick glasses. His hat had been shoved to the back of his head, making it look too small. His nearly invisible lips were moving silently, as if in prayer, and his left hand, matted with dark hair, was clutching a black velvet bag that presumably contained his prayer shawl and phylacteries.

Gate D 52 of Amsterdam's Schiphol Airport was manned by two Israeli security guards in shirtsleeves and several Dutch military policemen in navy-blue uniforms, armed with semiautomatics. With seeming nonchalance, like quality controllers in a factory, the Israelis inspected every passenger who stepped off the walkway. Only their eyes moved in their expressionless faces. Their leathery tans bore witness to a desert sun, just as the wrinkles around their eyes belied tense concentration.

The black-suited Hasid ahead of me strode past the security men without a glance. I thought I detected a trace of amusement in their eyes as he went by. They didn't seem to notice me at all. Shouldering my bag, which had already been examined in the departure lounge as well as in a special security area, I continued in his wake.

He plowed his way through a pile of suitcases and yellow tax-free shopping bags towards a plate-glass window facing east. Outside was a mammoth airplane that would soon swallow us up in its belly. Just before reaching the reflecting pane of glass, the Hasid untied his velvet pouch, carefully drew out his phylacteries, and put them on with practiced ease. He spread his prayer shawl as if he were about to set a table, kissed the fringes and the crown, and threw it over his broad shoulders.

He was surrounded by a group of similarly clad figures. Shrouded in their white *tallitim*, with little black leather boxes containing passages from the Scriptures on their foreheads, they bowed towards the east and swayed like ships' masts in a storm. Impervious to the noise in back of them, they chanted their prayers in a monotonous sing-song, with only an occasional plaintive wail. Dozens of Chagall-like rebbes and their mirrored images sent their prayers to heaven over the heads of the nervous and perspiring men, women, and children in the glossy green chairs.

The non-Jewish passengers gazed with barely disguised curiosity at this biblical scene – a foretaste of things to come. The others didn't even give it a second glance. After all, this extraordinary spectacle was part of their everyday lives. Only when the blond stewardesses arrived in their meticulous sky-blue uniforms did they sit up and take notice, following every movement in utter fascination. Unperturbed, the rebbes went on praying towards the big bird on the other side of the window. When they came to the end of the prayer, they tucked their *tallitim* and phylacteries back in their velvet pouches and chatted with each other as though they were standing in front of a synagogue instead of in the gleaming waiting room of a modern airport.

Thousands of feet above moss-green valleys, snow-capped mountains, and fleecy white clouds, the outwardly serene stewardesses started serving lunch. An aluminum-wrapped tray with the sticker of the Rabbinate of Amsterdam was handed to all the men wearing yarmulkes or hats, all the women whose kerchiefs or wigs betokened Orthodoxy, and anyone else who'd ordered kosher food.

. There was a commotion two rows ahead of me. The Talmud scholar with the graying black beard suddenly stood up. Towering over the seats, he held the foil-covered dish in his left hand and jabbed the forefinger of his right hand menacingly in the air.

He cautioned his students and fellow rabbis in Yiddish not to touch the food because he didn't know, and therefore didn't trust, the Dutch rabbi in charge of kosher certification. A flock of stewardesses gathered around him, and he spewed out his anger in English, accusing them of not having consulted him before leaving Amsterdam.

The purser attempted to clear a path through a mass of moon-faced, pale, and bespectacled yeshiva students, whose ritual fringes dangled beneath their white shirts and suspenders. But they had no intention of letting themselves be shoved aside. Curious as well as protective, they closed ranks around their rebbe. The uniformed attendant began to placate his agitated passenger and convince him that the kosher seal could be trusted. Gradually, the protest tapered off in volume. The Hasid mopped his red brow with a white handkerchief and allowed himself, still grumbling, to sink back into his seat.

Humming gently, the plane glided over Europe on a blanket of clouds. What with the vast stretch of white below and the immaculate blue dome above, time seemed to be suspended. For a few moments the war, which I carry around with me wherever I go, was reduced to a mere fraction of a second.

The couple seated next to me was on a pilgrimage to the Holy Land. Or so I gathered from the conversation between the woman, in her wash-and-wear dress and freshly permed hair, and the stewardess who brought a glass of water for the husband's medication. During the incident with the zealot, the man had gently shaken his head and chuckled indulgently.

Like me, they'd polished off their non-kosher meals without complaint. The sky-blue hostesses began collecting the picked-over trays and dirty dishes and placing them in their carts. The narrow aisle was hardly wide enough for the carts, much less passengers wanting to stretch their legs.

Suddenly, as if obeying an inner clock, dozens of men in black hats and suits or long black coats rose up from their seats, wriggled their way to the aisle, squeezed past the stewardesses and carts and gathered by the pantry and toilets. It was time for the *Mincha*, the afternoon prayer.

Bunched together, hat to hat, *tallit* to *tallit*, they rocked back and forth from west to east. Their murmured incantations resembled the dull drone of an organ's bass pipe.

The flustered stewardesses came to a halt by the tangled mass of people. They waited behind their carts, trying to maintain an air of politeness though their friendliness was clearly waning. In an attempt to check the flow, they asked the others to remain in their seats. Their request bounced off a wall of incomprehension. The determined men pushed their way to the aisle, where their brothers were already praying and swaying. The captain and the purser, under the erroneous impression that they had any influence, addressed the older, bearded Hasidim in loud, authoritarian voices, but their pleas fell on deaf ears. Their gold-striped uniforms, their talk of blocked aisles and danger might have been valid in another world, but not in that of the Talmud and the Torah.

I watched impassively, keeping my eyes on the clouds, the cabin, and *The New York Times*. The Hasidim embarrassed me, and I wanted to create the impression that I was different. That I was modern, cultured, maybe not even Jewish.

Beside me, an attractive, sturdily built stewardess, her cheeks flushed, her forehead and upper lip beaded with perspiration, was trying to navigate her cart past the thrusting thighs of her Orthodox passengers. The comforting remark offered by the pilgrims on my right was a bit too loud, a bit too clear: "If that isn't just like them." The stewardess laughed and agreed that she always had her hands full when "the sidelocks" were on board.

The words split the air like breaking ice. My ears heard "sidelocks," but my heart heard "Shylocks."

That word, filled with centuries of venom, touched a raw nerve. I was on my way to Israel, to the archives of Yad Vashem, where countless reports from ghettos and concentration camps were waiting for a pair of eyes to read them and bring their voices back to life. I too was irritated by the black-clad rebbes and their disregard for today's world, and yet we had a bond. Once, nearly forty years ago, in a barrack in Birkenau, we had shared the same fate. The bowing, the rocking, the dully mumbled Kaddish after selections: they were all buried somewhere in the Paleozoic of my memory.

Lod's arrival lounge reverberated with greetings and quarrels, laughter and tears, chatter and shouts above the *basso continuo* of the air conditioning.

Hasidic black faded among brightly colored shirts and blouses – there was only an occasional ink spot on the palette. Young soldiers with Uzis slung over their shoulders sauntered among the new arrivals.

A dark-eyed girl, almost coquettish in her tight uniform, checked my passport and asked in melodic sabra English what the purpose of my visit was. In reply I handed over a letter from Yad Vashem's well-known archivist: my passkey to the stories of my fellow concentration-camp survivors. She dropped her official mask and looked at me for a long time. Then she nodded and whispered, "*Mazel tov.*" I was in Israel.

The terminal's swinging door slammed shut behind me, and at once I was enveloped in a muggy laundry-room heat. I heaved my bags onto a hard-won luggage cart. The sidewalk was lined with men in shirtsleeves, some with skullcaps and some without, hoping to change "dol*lars*" into shekels and hissing exchange rates at me. Cabdrivers were standing in front of their beat-up cars, hustling customers, haggling over the price, and taking off in all directions with their vehicles fully loaded. I recognized the bus stop only because a bunch of passengers were waiting in the burning sun beside their bags and suitcases and grumbling about public transportation.

The antiquated Egged bus rattled and shook its way towards Jerusalem. The twin flaps of the hood trembled like a pair of flaring nostrils. Shekels danced on the coin counter beside the driver. I sat down next to the soldier assigned to guard the safety of the passengers and watched the butt of his rifle clank up and down on the worn metal floor like the hammer of a tinsmith. I tried to get a conversation going, but he was keeping an ostensibly relaxed though clearly vigilant eye on his surroundings, and he either didn't hear me or didn't want to. My voice was drowned out by a rousing symphony: the throb of the engine, the voices of the passengers arguing in a variety of languages, the Hebrew news reports blaring from the driver's radio.

The road to Jerusalem made a gradual climb past dusty red fields, groves of trees planted by friends of Israel, and craggy limestone bluffs. After that the road got steeper. The polyglot babel of the passengers could no longer be heard over the engine roar. My curiosity about everything inside and outside the bus began to shrivel in the heat and noise, and I was assailed by doubts about my trip.

Back home, surrounded by scores of books and bulging files, everything had seemed clear, plain, academic. Cool and outwardly detached, I'd asked myself questions about life and death in the camps as though I were an outsider. I'd hunted through files of yellowing, closely typed sheets of brittle postwar paper and read the reports of concentration-camp inmates who were strangers to me, because I was looking for answers to several questions: where had they been, how had they survived, and what had happened to them afterwards?

Now that I was on my way to the place where thousands of voices had been preserved so they could serve as witnesses for later generations, my objectivity was beginning to crumble. For the first time it occurred to me that I was going to have to project my own nightmare onto those of others. It was time for me to break out of my solitude and go in search of people who had known me and my parents or had seen us in one of the camps, as a way of exorcising my past.

I was jerked back to the present by the honking of horns in Jerusalem's modern suburbs. The sun shone down on the yellowish bricks of the houses and apartments, making them glisten like gold. The closed shutters gave the buildings an air of abandonment. But the streets were filled with women in gaily colored cotton dresses, men in short-sleeved shirts, and frolicking children. At the bus stop across from Herzl Park a swarm of bespectacled young men in black suits and broad-brimmed black hats – the uniform of Orthodox Jewry – waited outside their yeshiva. When a bus drove by without stopping, some of them angrily shook their fists. Were they so out of touch with the world, or did they consider themselves above all earthly rules?

The bus terminal on Jaffa Street was flanked by

nondescript, impersonal hotels made out of the same yellow blocks of stone. The station was filthy and menacing. Our bus screeched to a halt in the dirty loading area. The other buses roared and belched out exhaust. The drivers, their shirts soaked with sweat, were standing beside their vehicles, smoking, totally oblivious to the idling engines. I asked a few of them in English to tell me which bus went to the Old City, but they shrugged, or didn't even bother to do that much. I fared no better with Yiddish. At last, one pot-bellied driver inclined his head towards a group of noisy cabdrivers at the end of the overhang.

A feeling of loneliness crept over me, different and more intense than in other countries, because I'd expected to feel at home in the Promised Land. Instead, I was being treated like an outsider.

A line of impatient people had formed by the pay phones. The coin boxes were so close together that the callers had to put their hands over their ears to keep the conversation from being drowned out by the cacophony of voices and engines. Unsure of what to do, I lined up with the others and tried to buy some phone tokens, but no one had change for my crisp new banknotes. Seeing my predicament, an old lady with a sunlined face and a skin that testified to years of outdoor work simply handed me a token and asked in Yiddish: "Where do you come from?" Her Golda Meir face lit up – a native who wasn't hostile.

The token took me out of my isolation. The voice at the other end of the receiver belonged to my friend Zwi: my point of reference in Israel. A short, highly respected surgeon, Zwi had the strength and resilience of a coil of steel. During the war he'd escaped from the Dutch internment camp of Westerbork. Later, in the turbulent Palestine of 1945, he'd joined the Haganah. Since then, we'd seen each other only briefly at infrequent intervals. Zwi was a fiery patriot who defended Israel's hard-line politics with dogged determination, and I was a vacillating doubter at a comfortable distance from the troubles, so our discussions usually ended in a stalemate.

His enthusiastic *shalom* reverberated through the receiver. He gave me short, clear instructions for the cab-driver. His house, located in the Old City, was beyond the reach of modern transportation. His address didn't conjure up any images: during my last visit, before the Six-Day War, this part of Jerusalem had belonged to Jordan.

I climbed into the taxi behind the cabbie's damp back. Arab music boomed from the radio. I sat on the edge of my seat so as not to miss the breathtaking images outside the dilapidated cab: Coptic clerics with their hair in thick knots, Greek Orthodox priests in black robes and stove-pipe hats, swan-like nuns in white wimples, Hasidim in somber black, Arabs in flapping djellabas and white keffi-yehs that effectively protected them from the sun, and Israelis in European summer wear, with and without yar-mulkes, which were often no bigger than the tonsures of the brown-robed Franciscans. With the weather-beaten walls of the City of David as a backdrop, the representa-tives of the world's religions passed each other like ships in the night, in seeming harmony.

The cab came to stop in the middle of a construction site. The driver gestured irritably that this was the end of my journey and that the address, which I once again shoved under his nose, was somewhere behind an unfinished apartment complex. I found myself standing helplessly with my suitcase and overnight bag amid cement mixers, mounds of glistening yellow bricks, sacks of cement, and piles of sand.

I asked two passersby for directions, but they didn't seem to know the street. The Old City was *terra incognita*. However, the moment I mentioned my host's name and profession, they dropped their callous indifference. Speaking sabra English, they guided me to a narrow alley that had been modernized, and yet it looked so old that I might have been back in the days before the destruction of the Temple.

Zwi was standing in the doorway. Twenty years had added only a little silver to his hair. Once again I was reminded of steel, but then dented on the anvil of time. We hugged each other, and I could see in his eyes that there had been too many wars in the intervening years. But he didn't utter a word of complaint. His welcoming cheer revealed nothing of the deep-seated problems that beset his country daily.

He addressed my guides in rapid Hebrew. I recognized a few Dutch place-names: my temporary admission to Israeli society. We took a short stroll down the street, which was so narrow I could stretch my arms out and almost touch the houses on either side. The restoration had been done so well that it sent my imagination soaring. His house, likewise made of golden-yellow sandstone, had a heavy bronze door and grilled windows. Across the street was a little shop filled with Torah scrolls, long rows of Talmudic texts, menorahs, Shabbes candlesticks, shofars, velvet challah covers and silver Kiddush cups.

Michelangelo's Moses was standing in the doorway, dressed in a black silk caftan, with a pair of thick oval eyeglasses on his nose. Until now the age of the kings and prophets had been nothing but words on yellowed paper. Suddenly it seemed more real than the space age.

In Zwi's house, antiquity merged with the present. There was a modern, Dutch-like interior, but the walls must have been at least ten inches thick. The steps of the inner courtyard looked like they'd been hewn from stone. Zwi's wife Hefzi was waiting at the top. A native-born Israeli with hair and eyes as black as Esther's, Hefzi had acquired her PhD and Hebrew-accented Dutch in Utrecht. She welcomed me with the ease of a sabra who looks upon the Diaspora as a thing of the past.

Zwi's study was an enclave of Western erudition: row after row of books on a wide range of subjects and several recent watercolors of his beloved Old City in exotic colors. Looking out the window, I saw Zwi standing on the rooftop. The pale slabs of stone had been smoothed down to form a terrace, which was lined with plants typical of southern climes – thick leaves, thorns, and bright colors. He gestured for me to join him.

A miracle unveiled itself with every step I took. By the time I reached Zwi, the Wailing Wall had been revealed in all its glory. A religious awe I didn't even know I possessed rendered me speechless. The cradle of history lay at my feet.

The huge, weather-beaten sandstone blocks were directly in front of me, though several hundred yards away. I could see Hasidim in caftans and round hats or fur-lined *shtreimel* bowing frenetically or rocking to and fro. Others were reading Torah rolls on tables placed there for that purpose. Men in conventional clothes, caught up by the religious fervor, were also bowing and rocking. Women whose heads and faces were hidden by dark shawls and whose prayer books were almost invisible in the folds of their dresses were bending like reeds before the holy stones. The square in front of the Wailing Wall was teeming with camera-slung tourists, their heads covered with everything imaginable. Young Uzi-toting Israeli soldiers were patrolling the area. Hyper-alert under an easy exterior, they were protecting believers and non-believers alike.

By looking through Zwi's binoculars, I could see the pious and the credulous stuffing slips of paper into the crevices between the worn blocks of Solomon's former temple. I couldn't help wondering irreverently whether Yahweh responded better to the written or the spoken word.

The evening sun reflected off the golden cupola of the Dome of the Rock. Though I knew that enmity lurked in the garden of this Islamic shrine, I was overwhelmed by its beauty and regretted the divisiveness. In the distance, the spires of the Christian churches were silhouetted against the sky like the swords of ruthless Crusaders, menacing and unapproachable.

Still speechless, I greedily soaked up the images. The spell was broken only by repeated calls to dinner. As we ate, my friends plied me with local politics, discussing problems I'd only vaguely read about in faraway Holland. Since my head was still spinning from the trip, impressions flickered by like tropical fish in an aquarium, and my interest in politics was even more lukewarm than usual.

During dessert, I tiredly outlined my plans. Despite

their long day in the clinic and laboratory, Zwi and Hefzi
were discerning and quick to understand. They pressed
for details. It was late, but Zwi ignored my weak protests
and phoned the archivist of Yad Vashem to arrange an
appointment for me for the following morning.

In the guest bedroom, I fell into a dreamless sleep from
which I was awakened at sunrise by the deafening call of
the muezzin from the Al Aqsa mosque. My hours as a
tourist had come to an end.

In the tingling coolness of Jerusalem's early-morning air, I
waited for the bus amid a group of squawking schoolboys
with yarmulkes. When the noise became unbearable,
women with grocery bags shrieked "*Sheket*," but their
pleas for quiet had little effect. The youngsters hurled
themselves through the half-open doors of the shuddering
bus with whoops and hollers.

The men perusing their newspapers, the housewives
on their way to the market, the Hasidim mumbling their
prayers or hotly debating some issue or another – the
passengers all glanced up in momentary alarm but didn't
get angry. The generation in which they'd placed their
hopes was surrounded by kindly indulgence and the hint
of a smile.

Every morning except Saturday, I watched the city flash
by my window. I even began to recognize the faces of my
fellow commuters; I'd become a resident among other
residents, an inhabitant who didn't speak the language.

My stop was marked by a towering red work of art.
Each time I walked by I wondered, rather defiantly, why
Alexander Calder had decided to call his lonely steel
artwork at the entryway to Yad Vashem *Roots*.

The parking lot in front of the modest archives wing was empty except for a few bus loads of solemn-faced tourists, the first that day to view the life-size photographs epitomizing the years of our horror.

Together with the staff, who'd welcomed me with friendly professionalism, I entered the building through the side entrance, as if I'd worked there for years. My footsteps resounded on the spiral staircase like the tolling of a bell, but once I closed the door of Gideon Hausner's sparsely furnished office behind me, I was surrounded by the silence of a solitary-confinement cell.

Twenty years after Eichmann's execution, I found myself seated at the desk where Hausner, the public prosecutor in the Eichmann trial, had examined stacks of incriminating documents. On the white wall facing me was a huge map covered with more than three thousand dots representing the inviting, romantic names of places that were nightmares in the Third Reich. In front of me were files and tapes containing the reports of men and women for whom the dots were synonymous with humiliation and murder, with hunger and exhaustion.

Day after day, thousands of words flashed by me, conjuring up images of endless lines of emaciated prisoners in rags, of well-fed kapos with clubs and bellowing *Blockältesten*,* of boxcars under a burning sun or an icy blizzard, of expressionless SS guards with their rifles cocked, as if they were at a clay-pigeon shoot.

I told myself that I was simply doing research, that I was supposed to be looking for a common denominator. My

---

* Literally "Block Elders." Prisoners appointed to oversee a row of barracks.

face was tense. In the cafeteria, I joined in conversations mechanically. I felt like I was having an awful dream in which nobody could reach me because there was a wall of glass between us. A nameless fear kept me from visiting the museum and saying Kaddish in the memorial shrine.

I waited at the bus stop again every evening. Crowded buses whizzed by, one after another, to the angry jeers of the yeshiva students. The scene had become familiar: the two weeks since my arrival seemed like years.

I was staying with two elderly sabras who pointed with pride to several generations of ancestors born in what was then Palestine. She, round and brimming with hospitality, chatty and astute, kept a close watch on my well-being. Food, and plenty of it, was her remedy against all ills. A sense of piety may have prompted her to accept my raking up the past, but as far as she was concerned, today and tomorrow always come first.

He, Moische, a stocky man with the muscles of a pioneer for whom no burden was ever too heavy, was enamored of TV news, which poured in from Amman, Jerusalem, and Cairo in a steady stream. When the last picture had faded away and the only sound was the whir of the fan, he sometimes began to talk about the past, in hesitant but unadulterated Yiddish. Pogroms in Vilnius, skirmishes with the Turks and the English, friendship and enmity with the Arabs, the early years of statehood, the wars. But never the Shoah, history's unhealed wound.

The stacks of documents in front of me began to swell, and my head began to fill with more and more facts . . . and more and more chaos. I'd become the Sorcerer's Apprentice, unable to keep up with the flow of paper and not knowing the magic word that would make everything fall into place. I began to lose sight of my objective, since every story was so unique and each case governed by so much chance that any attempt at generalization seemed like a desecration.

Confused, I wandered through the building, past countless rows of books and over the grounds of Yad Vashem, where the mocking sun beat down on my bare head. I sought the shade of the trees that Israel had planted as a tribute to Righteous Gentiles and suddenly found myself in front of the memorial shrine.

An elderly man with gray hair and a deeply lined face gave me a searching look with the one eye he had left, handed me a yarmulke, and asked me in Yiddish, not beating around the bush, "Which one were you in?" We exchanged the names of concentration camps as if they were tokens. He ushered me into a darkened room, where I was surrounded by stone and space. An eternal flame burned amid the accursed names of camps. I whispered them as a malediction, and an old, unbearable sense of abandonment triggered my tears. With my shoulders heaving, I stared into the fire and mumbled Kaddish, like a timid child unsure of his prayers.

I found myself back in the blinding sunlight, my armor visibly shattered. The old man nodded in understanding. I finally knew what I was looking for.

The short, usually bustling archivist was sitting quietly behind his desk. Gone was the cool, academic detachment that had so far characterized our brief conversations in his office. He gazed at me with a penetrating but almost fatherly look. I gave him a concise account of my arrest, the camps I had been in, and my homecoming. He recognized the bits and pieces of his own story, as well as that of the hundreds of other stories in the metal filing cabinets around him. He knew, he told me gently, what the frenetic search of his visitors meant. Some tried to ferret out the names of relatives, friends, and fellow prisoners, while others attempted to shed light on the black curtain in their memories. But to us all, Yad Vashem was a vast graveyard without tombstones.

Frowning, he stared into space. Then he abruptly got to his feet and opened a steel cabinet. The door trembled like the aftermath of a thunderstorm. With unfailing accuracy, he grabbed a stack of faded files, bulging with closely typed carbon copies, and laid it down in front of me so that I could read the title, in bold black letters: AUSCHWITZ TRIAL, FRANKFURT/MAIN 1964, I.

I looked at the words in surprise and felt ashamed of my ignorance. At the time, I'd blocked out the trial and buried myself in such totally different work that the folders now filled me with fear. I took them in my arms with a feeling akin to reverence. Propelled by impatience and a premonition, I took my place by Gideon Hausner's map. After a dozen single-spaced legal-sized sheets, I found myself once again behind the barbed wire of Birkenau.

The man whose account I was reading was a year younger than I was. I could only vaguely picture his birthplace, Ostrava, which at that time lay in the heart of Europe. My egocentric notion that Prague was the last outpost of civilization was disproved on the first page. Ostrava turned out to be a large industrial center on Czechoslovakia's Polish border, and Yehuda B., born to a family of Jewish manufacturers, grew up there in comfortable circumstances. At his family's dining table, refugees

seeking safety in the East told of the roundups and concentration camps in the West.

In 1941 the Jews of Ostrava, like those in Holland, were
ordered out of the schools. Underground classes were
organized. Small groups of children would meet in a
variety of living rooms, moving on to the next one when
betrayal seemed imminent. Reading and writing were
taught by scholars who'd been barred from working in
their fields but found satisfaction in educating the young.

One by one the teachers were sent to the East, where
they disappeared without a trace. The children stopped
going to classes. Families fled or were rounded up. Ter-
rifying reports of deportations trickled in from Prague and
Brno like vitriol.

A package arrived from Auschwitz: the suspenders of a
popular teacher. It was accompanied by a letter
demanding that the postage be paid, as otherwise they
would not send his ashes.

Postcards with veiled references to hunger and suffering arrived from Theresienstadt, a transit camp for Jews
from all over Europe, and then the callups began. In the
two days between the order and the deportation, many
old people preferred to take their own lives. The more
hopeful attempted to obtain documents stating that they
had Aryan ancestors. Others went in search of food,
durable clothing, and shoes, keeping up their spirits by
interpreting the rumors in the most optimistic light.

Yehuda's description of his arrival in the Theresienstadt
ghetto awakened my own dormant images: the ramparts
and battlements of this onetime fortress; the gray and
red rooftops of the neglected, cavernous barracks; the
arcades overlooking the cobblestoned parade grounds;

the prisoners in wrinkled clothes lugging their battered suitcases and anxiously averting their eyes from the gend-armes and SS guards; the long, straight rows of nearly deserted streets, lined with dilapidated buildings whose paint was peeling like charred skin; the emaciated faces of the ghetto-dwellers behind the dirt-caked windows, their eyes glazed and focused inward; the Jewish officials humbly removing their caps for anyone in a uniform.

Yehuda's report made this run-down, overcrowded gar-rison town – built in the time of the Hapsburgs – come to life. I saw the crowded bunks in the drafty rooms, where having a nail to hang your moldy clothes on was con-sidered a luxury. The lines of men and women, aged before their time, waiting resignedly before the cauldrons of thin gray soup or crumbling chunks of bread, measuring each other's portions with looks of distrust, their deep-set eyes burning with hunger and envy. The boys and girls who'd found alternative ways to sup-plement the meager rations watching in barely disguised contempt as their elders begged for more or argued over the division of the food.

I didn't know it at the time, but Theresienstadt had dormitories known as youth houses, in which children were grouped according to age and nationality. They were secretly given lessons by idealistic teachers and youth leaders attempting to boost the morale of their pupils and shield them from the misery of the ghetto.

Nor was I aware of the cultural life that blossomed in the basements and attics of Theresienstadt, despite the repression. Musicians composed, trained their younger colleagues, gave concerts, and played chamber music on instruments smuggled into the camp. Artists did their best to keep on painting, drawing, and sculpting, even if it meant working between the rows of bunk beds and drying underwear.

Nearly two years after Yehuda, I arrived in Theresienstadt from the Dutch camp of Westerbork, glassy-eyed and incapable of understanding the shadowy world around me. By that time the majority of the artists had either starved to death or been transported to their final destination in the East. The stage sets of the children's opera *Brundibar* and Smetana's *Bartered Bride* had long ago gone up in the flames of rusty cast-iron stoves.

Yehuda's deportation to Auschwitz-Birkenau in December 1943 had put an end to a period of absurd contradictions, one in which well-known educators had attempted, on the eve of destruction, to pass on their knowledge and skills to the children in the youth houses. Despite the many hardships, Yehuda had learned how to draw and paint. Famous artists, using paper obtained through clandestine channels, had fostered his talent and left a lasting impression.

With mounting anxiety, I read Yehuda's account of his transport to Birkenau's "Family Camp" B II B: a long ride in a dark cattle car that ended in the nighttime glare of searchlights illuminating a scene engraved as sharply on my brain as it was on his. Yehuda's description of life in the camp – the selections, the gassings, the thousands of new arrivals from Theresienstadt in March 1944, and the May transports carrying me and my parents – gave me the feeling that he and I were looking through one pair of eyes.

Mesmerized, I read on. His story paralleled mine like two sets of railroad tracks. They converged in the beginning of 1944, during the last selection in the doomed Family Camp. At that moment we found ourselves standing in front of Mengele along with more than a hundred other boys, all of us naked and rigid with fear.

Yehuda's words branded themselves on my retina. I saw what he saw, what I saw. I went on reading through my tears and recognized every detail. A feeling of gratitude and joy welled up inside me. "He survived. Oh God, let him still be alive!"

Without reading to the end, I raced into the corridor like one possessed, hoping to find my wise adviser, the archivist. After all, he'd known what I was looking for. With almost childlike faith, I assumed he'd know the whereabouts of the person I'd thought was dead.

Once again I found myself seated in his office. It seemed like a month instead of twenty-four hours since I'd last spoken to him. He raised his eyebrows and asked whether I'd already worked my way through the entire file. Stumbling over my words, I told him of my discovery. He put up his hand to check my excited account, and a nearly imperceptible smile crossed his face. He came right to the point: "And now you want to know if he's still alive?"

Unable to speak, I nodded and read the answer from his lips before the words were even out of his mouth.

Yehuda is alive. He's a well-known artist, he lives in Jerusalem, he's in good health, he's married and has children, he's recorded our past in oil paintings and pencil sketches, and he's a good friend who's always welcome in Yad Vashem.

On the other end of the line I hear a quiet male voice whose harsh Hebrew vowels are softened by a Central

European accent. My hesitant introduction in German seems out of place, but I don't know what else to do. I hear a quick intake of breath. I talk into the cupped palm of my hand, groping for words. Words meant for his ears only. Anyone else might not understand. He breaks in after only a few sentences. Velvety Czechoslovakian German, hoarse with emotion, impatient, as if the phone is an irritating obstacle.

We have to see each other, talk to each other, without delay.

He dictates his address, tries to explain how to find his house, gets mixed up, and urges me to take a taxi.

The conversation of the chatty cabdriver burbles past me. My mind is on other matters. We drive through a sweltering neighborhood of palm trees and prewar housing that's apparently escaped the notice of Jerusalem's building-code inspectors.

The cabbie hesitates, stops to ask a lone pedestrian for directions, and gets even more entangled in the labyrinth of streets. He finally stops the car and indicates that I should continue on foot. His professional pride prevents him from accepting a tip.

Once the cab is gone, I'm surrounded by the silence of the siesta. The cicadas singing in the trembling heat merely accentuate the quiet. I try to muffle my footsteps. To shield my head from the sun, I put on a kibbutz hat, but it's too small. I peer intently at street signs and house numbers tucked behind bougainvillea bushes. My heart is pounding at the thought of seeing Yehuda, or of getting so hopelessly lost in the confusing tangle of streets that I won't see him at all.

All of a sudden I'm standing in front of a house with a lopsided grape arbor that fits Yehuda's description. A little white dog is lying in the shadow, twitching in his sleep.

For a moment I hesitate to put the wheels of time back into motion. But I take a deep breath and ring the doorbell. The dog, startled out of his sleep, breaks the silence with his shrill barking. "*Sheket, sheket,*" a male voice shouts from the side of the house. I can't see anyone, but I hear my name being called in a deep, questioning voice: "Gerhard?" I move in the direction of the voice and see him standing there. A slight figure with lively blue eyes, an almost boyish face, and a full head of hair with just a touch of gray. He comes towards me with his arms outstretched: "Gerhard!" Then eagerly, his voice higher, "*Shalom, shalom!*" My eyes grow moist. I search his face for features I remember from forty years ago, a vague portrait in the forlorn frame of the camp. He looks at me . . . searches . . . then finds what he's looking for. His eyes light up in recognition: "It's you! I remember you and the other three Dutch boys!"

We throw our arms around each other. For a moment we clench our jaws and say nothing, almost ashamed of our strong emotions.

The house is dark – the Venetian blinds have been lowered to keep out the sun. He pours me a soda and showers me with fruit and candy, postponing the moment we'll have to swap stories. When he's run out of things to do, he perches on the edge of the couch, his hands on his knees, his eyes focused intently on my mouth. "Tell me, tell me everything!" he says. He listens with equal intensity. When our stories overlap, he fills in gaps, corrects me. He dares to put into words scenes that had become unspeakable nightmares to me. In my presence, he allows himself to see images he'd blocked out before. His "Do you remember?" makes us laugh or, more often, cry. We trade memories the way other people trade postage stamps.

After liberation, our lives diverged again. In the lonely years of poverty after the war, we'd sought different ways to put the horror behind us. Forgetting or acceptance was out of the question, even if we'd wanted to. Neither his art nor my academic career could erase the scars of our youth. I went in search of background information, causes, explanations. Yehuda went in search of images, pictures . . . and people. He stuns me by announcing that he'd found other survivors of our "group," by which he means the group of boys whom fate had thrown together in Men's Camp B II D when the Family Camp in Birkenau was liquidated. I knew of only two other survivors besides myself, but Yehuda had turned up fifteen more. With almost a note of triumph, he lists their names, places of residence, continent.

They were boys then, and now they're middle-aged men. They write letters and talk to each other from time to time. The past is a vault that is seldom opened. The youngest of the group, Dov K., is a historian. Like Yehuda, he'd been one of the main witnesses in the 1964 Auschwitz trial in Frankfurt.

Yehuda picks up the phone to call him. He's so nervous that his fingers fumble over the dial. It takes a few tries, but he finally gets through. Hoarse and stumbling over his words, he tells Dov that I'm here.

Seated in a tweed-covered armchair, I wait for Dov in the faculty lounge of an Israeli university. The room overlooks a pond with a gently gurgling fountain, and some of the staff are sitting outside in lawn chairs. Their educated murmurs help soothe my jangled nerves. It's not just the prospect of seeing a fellow camp inmate after thirty-eight years that's put them on edge, but also the unexpected weapons search at the entrance to the campus.

I'd gotten off the bus at the main gate along with a horde of students in T-shirts and jeans, some of them chattering in groups and others engrossed in their books or newspapers. We'd joined the long lines of people waiting to be frisked, as if all this was perfectly normal.

Sooner than expected, I'd found myself at one of three glassed-in booths where Uzi-armed guards were checking coats and briefcases with metal detectors. Nobody was grumbling, or at any rate not that I could see. Everyone was being subjected to a rapid, routine search. They answered the questions and calmly moved on as though this was the most ordinary thing in the world.

The line had come to a halt with me. I didn't understand a word of the young soldier's Hebrew, and he looked blank when I replied in English. He poked in my papers, frisked me and started to open my tape recorder. At that point the woman in back of me offered to translate. The soldier asked what my business at the university was and who I had an appointment with. He kept firing questions at me – whether out of curiosity or distrust I didn't know.

The line, shaken out of its lethargy, began to get restless. Voices urged the guards to snap it up. Finally an older man had shuffled over, taken charge of the interrogation, freed me from the claws of misunderstanding, and escorted me to the lounge.

Seated in my comfortable armchair, I realize that while this university may look like those in Holland, it's different.

My eyes explore the face of every middle-aged man I see. I intuitively feel that none of them is Dov.

I wait, absent-mindedly scanning a newspaper and trying to look inconspicuous.

A shadow falls on the paper, and an uncertain voice inquires: "Gerhard?" I look up, sure it's Dov, though I don't recognize him. The two of us are overcome with shyness. We shake hands, rather formally: one researcher to another, wary of emotions, in a setting that doesn't understand, *can't* understand, what binds us together.

We walk over to the faculty dining room, and next to him I feel embarrassingly tall. In a flash I see him as he used to be: the youngest – and smallest – of our group.

He waves to friends, explains the items on the menu, and orders lunch from a pretty Yemenite waitress. In the familiar surroundings of a university dining hall the tension lifts. We talk about our work, studiously avoiding the past as if to protect our food.

Outside, out of sight of students and co-workers, our conversation returns to more weighty matters. He listens intently to my tale of poring through archives and trial records, alert to every name, every fact. He interrupts occasionally to fill in a gap, pose a question, make a suggestion. Emotion gradually takes the place of academic detachment. In a quiet voice he describes his search for documents about Auschwitz, Eichmann, and anything else directly or indirectly related to our personal histories. He's modest about his finds in the ocean of papers in German and American war archives, but I know how valuable they are.

There's a sudden burst of activity around us. We've lost track of time. Unfortunately, Dov can't keep his students waiting any longer. Torn between duty and catharsis, he opts for the here and now. We get up stiffly from our cramped positions, but are unwilling and unable to say good-bye. At almost the same moment we both realize that we must go on, that we must record our talks, that we must pass our knowledge on to others. We agree to meet the next day at the house of our mutual friend Yehuda, the painter, so that the three of us can delve into our past.

Once more I find myself in a car. But this time I'm sitting next to Dov, who knows the way through the silent streets shimmering in the heat. Once more the white dog wakes up and shatters the siesta with his barking. Once more Yehuda shouts "*Sheket*," but this time his voice is familiar and full of welcome.

He guides us through the darkened living room to his studio so we won't be disturbed by his sons when they come home from school.

"I'm afraid my studio isn't very large," he apologizes. There isn't an easel in sight. Instead, the shelves are piled with paper, portfolios, and woodblocks. His love of graphic art is clear from the lack of paint tubes, brushes, stains, the smell of oil and turpentine – the usual artistic clutter. Three straight-backed chairs are grouped in a circle as if a string trio is about to play. Dov and I, accompanied by the clumsy tinkle of glasses in the kitchen, install ourselves and our instruments: our tape recorders. This way, we can register our words, and our silences, as we talk about then and about now.

Dov, to my left, is outwardly calm. Despite the heat, he hasn't removed the jacket of his seersucker suit. He keeps a watchful eye on his Sony, though it's running smoothly. His face is pale, his breathing fast. Yehuda, across from me, wearing a short-sleeved, open-necked shirt, is excited, almost cheerful. A large, crudely tattooed number is visible on his left forearm. He looks at us in childlike wonder and suggests we get started.

My heart is pounding; I can't say a word. Stage fright has got my tongue. Dov's voice appears to come out of nowhere, soft, hesitant. He apparently deals with the tension by clinging to the role of professor: "For a long time Gerhard thought only three boys from our group had survived the war. It might be useful to examine this matter in more detail. Perhaps we should begin by stating our names, giving a brief biography, and introducing ourselves."

The realization that this conversation isn't going to be confined to these four walls puts a damper on things. I hear myself droning my personal history in short, crisp telegraphese: names, dates, camps. Dov, his voice hoarse and faint, says even less. Yehuda regrets the restraint, but follows our lead.

A reticent Dov addresses us and our absent listeners in long, carefully formulated sentences: "If I may, I'd like to propose that we limit ourselves to one particular aspect, namely the group of boys between the ages of thirteen and sixteen who were together with us in Birkenau in 1944. This is the reason the three of us decided to meet here in Yehuda's house in Jerusalem in 1982." I nod my assent, though his academic formalism has thrown me off balance.

He continues: "Gerhard came to Israel to research the question of how people could survive the camps, but after he met us he decided to narrow it down to our own experiences. Almost one fifth of the group of boys who passed the last selection in Birkenau's Family Camp lived to see liberation, in spite of the horrendous circumstances. Why did such a large percentage survive? Gerhard was surprised to hear from Yehuda and me that there were about twenty of us left. We asked ourselves whether there was an explanation for the higher percentage of survivors in our group compared to that of the adult prisoners, and I realized that I'd never given it a thought before."

An agitated Yehuda, his hands cupped as if they contain a bowlful of answers, adds: "Don't forget that there were hundreds of boys in the Family Camp, but that only eighty-nine of us made it through Mengele's selection in July 1944. All the others were annihilated. Besides that, the hardship didn't rain down on us all at once, but came drop by drop. In that sense we were unlike the French, who usually arrived in Auschwitz directly from Drancy in Paris. From house to hell with nothing in between. Those of us in the camps who'd managed to stay alive until then had built up a kind of immunity, despite the constant hunger."

Yehuda's argument, emotional and analytical at the same time, catches me by surprise, and I make no attempt to interrupt.

"Up till 1944 our physical condition hadn't been undermined by unbearably heavy work. In the Men's Camp in

Birkenau we even had shoes and clothes. And sometimes even pills for diarrhea. Don't forget: diarrhea meant death, lice meant death, and floggings and beatings meant death if you weren't given a chance to recover. Aside from the selections for the gas chambers and other forms of annihilation, our physical circumstances were somewhat better than those of the older Jewish prisoners. Mentally, we might have been a little better off too. We weren't quite as dehumanized as the men who'd been there longer, because many of us had parents and relatives who'd managed to stay alive until July 1944."

Still outwardly cool and collected, like a teacher in a classroom, Dov proceeds to point out the weakness in Yehuda's argument, giving specific examples. I listen, participating and yet keeping my distance. The studio, the heat, the friendly discussion: reality fades, time passes.

"When you said 'drop by drop,'" Dov replies, "I suppose you were referring to the Family Camp in Birkenau, which housed the transports from Theresienstadt. The conditions in the Family Camp weren't as bad, because the Germans were planning on using it to pull the wool over the eyes of the Red Cross if it insisted on an inspection. As for our mental state, I'm not so sure it was better. After all, the mechanism of destruction was being carried out daily right before our eyes, so we knew what was in store for us. We just thought we'd been given a short reprieve."

"That's because the hunting season in the Family Camp was declared every six months," Yehuda remarks. "It was known as *Sonderbehandlung*."*

* Literally "special treatment." A Nazi code term for extermination.

"But," Dov says with visible emotion, "we were convinced that we were going to meet the same fate."

The glass shell of his detachment is beginning to crack. "I just remembered something else," he adds. "The absurdity of the atmosphere in the children's barracks. We even had a kind of cabaret show full of gallows humor. Gruesome jokes in which SS men carried out selections and lice checks in heaven, as if Auschwitz kept on going into eternity."

Yehuda nods emphatically. "Don't forget that we were young. The camps were practically the only reality we knew. We accepted almost without question the idea that we could be exterminated like vermin. We were unable to conceive of a normal childhood outside of Auschwitz."

I interrupt to point out that we'd actually had a kind of schizophrenic concept of reality, but Dov corrects me immediately. "Maybe you still remembered what normal life was like, but the younger kids – and I was nearly five years younger than you and three years younger than Yehuda – hadn't had time to form a fixed idea of the civilized world. As far as we were concerned, Theresienstadt or Auschwitz was the world, though it was far from civilized."

I start summarizing our conversation up to now in hopes of getting us back on the track, but Dov's comment about our ages has stuck in my mind. I'd been fifteen at the time, almost sixteen. No longer a child, not yet an adult. Caught in the no-man's-land between the gas chamber and the labor transports – saved by chance. I force myself to focus on the present discussion, to pick up the thread of the conversation, to concentrate on empirical facts, seeking shelter in rational thought.

As I toss out a few theories, my friends nod in agreement. I hear myself describing the years of experience we'd acquired in other camps before we ever arrived in Auschwitz as a "social learning process," and it sounds ridiculous. But I use it to shield myself from painful memories.

We'd picked up some strange skills behind barbed wire: we were experts in mimicry, alert as wild animals to the presence of hunters. No guard ever surprised us when we were resting to conserve our energy. We jumped to attention like model soldiers, whipped off our caps, answered in crisp German. We knew the codes and camp ethics without having been taught. We never looked the SS in the eye, we did our best to stick together, and we tried to keep each other from the abyss of apathy. We were adept at "organizing" food and anything else we could lay our hands on, but we never stole from our buddies: the iron-clad rule of the camps.

The shock of arriving at night amid electrified fences; the shouts of men in uniforms, armed with guns and clubs; the relentless searchlights; the throbbing engines of the trucks. Many of the people who came directly from the outside world, from their own homes, were plunged into either passive resignation or protective madness. Were we youngsters better equipped to deal with the initial shock? Had we shut ourselves off from reality? Had we realized what was happening around us?

As I talk, it dawns on me that, in the first few weeks after my arrival, I'd wrapped myself in a protective cloak. I'd looked, but hadn't seen. I'd heard, but hadn't understood. I'd been eager to believe that the smoke came from factories, that the shower heads were real.

Dov nods in compassionate understanding: "Those of us who arrived a few months earlier and had survived the first *Sonderbehandlung* knew better. We thought the same thing when we first got there, that our eyes and ears were deceiving us. Flames, day after day, trains, long lines of people, olive-green trucks: bit by bit our fantasy was torn to shreds. I spent hours staring at the flames and trying to imagine how the body of a human being could be changed into smoke."

His voice gets hoarser, softer. His words begin to flow faster and faster, as if he can't hold them back. "One thing keeps recurring in my dreams – the sense of inevitability, the knowledge that you can't escape. I was living with death all around me; I was constantly afraid of dying. I didn't have a single ray of hope. Even when the front was getting closer and we could hear the roar of the cannons, I still couldn't imagine being freed from the iron grip of Birkenau. I thought the tanks would arrive too late to save us. I also thought it was childish to fantasize about liberation because I was absolutely convinced that our fate was sealed."

Dov hesitates and glances at us, as if to reassure himself of our sympathy before going on: "I still have the same dream. I'm standing in the crematorium in the middle of a big group of children. I hide and manage to escape. I even make it outside the camp. Then I find myself in a train station, and a voice from a loudspeaker suddenly calls my name. They grab me and take me back to the crematorium. In my dream I'm sure that every time I try to escape, they'll catch me."

A silence falls, and then he adds, pensively, "When I think about it now, I wonder which was better: accepting reality or blocking it out. The fear I felt back then, that dream . . . it still haunts me."

Yehuda's head bobs up and down, confirming that he has the same nightmares. "I always think, 'You won't get away with it, not this time.' Afterwards I wonder if it has something to do with guilt. But about what? And towards whom? After all, what did we kids do wrong except live? Sitting there on our bunks, we were like a small family. Together with the other boys in our group, we were one big family. We helped each other whenever we could, and that must have increased our chances of survival. When we were in the Men's Camp, the rest of the camp was the outside world. Out there it was okay to steal, but you helped your buddies. Once we even sacrificed a bread ration to buy an aspirin for a sick comrade. We didn't feel quite as lost as the older prisoners. Nor did we have to rely on our own resources quite as much. We still had someone to talk to, someone to share our memories with. Maybe that's why we wanted to help other children. Those kids who arrived on a transport from the Lodz ghetto, for example. They were put in Camp E, on the other side of the barbed wire, and we threw them bits of bread, spoons, whatever we could spare, even though the guards in the watchtowers fired warning shots."

Excited, nearly out of breath, he continues: "I remember a boy who stole some bread from a woman in the Women's Camp who still had her child with her. That was rare, practically a miracle. We didn't talk to him for days. He sold himself to a *Blockältester* for bread, and used that to try to get back in our good graces. He died soon after liberation, from overeating and food poisoning."

I have the uneasy feeling that he's "romanticized" the camaraderie. The glow of solidarity was tarnished for me by what I perceived to be an almost unbridgeable gap between nationalities and languages. But I hold my tongue. Who's to say how much is memory and how much solace?

Yehuda's flood of associations can no longer be checked. "Some of the boys tried to escape reality. Whenever we were ordered to take a load of wood or tar paper to the crematorium, they'd try to switch places with someone else. Or they'd shut their eyes when we went past the gallows. Those of us who'd arrived from Theresienstadt a few months earlier were more curious, more realistic. In retrospect, I don't know which was better. A dream world was dangerous, but so was reality. I guess people instinctively chose whatever suited them best."

Dov, staring reflectively into space, says, "You know, it's funny, but a few nice moments have stuck in my memory as well. Like the white stripes in the blue sky that the bombers made when they flew over the camp. Or my crush on a girl in the Women's Camp who was totally beyond my reach. The mountains on the horizon. The moment, a few weeks after we were liberated, when Misha G.'s father found him in the hospital and took him to England."

"I suppose everyone looks back on his childhood as a lost paradise," Yehuda philosophizes. "Childhood is childhood, no matter how paradoxical that may sound. Even though it was so horrible, I still say to myself: 'Thank God I've had this experience.' You tend to romanticize everything you saw and went through as a child." He raises his arms in the air and scoffs theatrically: "I was in

Theresienstadt, Auschwitz, and Mauthausen – like a soldier boasting that he was on this front, that front, and that front."

Dov replies that he never felt like that. His father had been one of Auschwitz's first prisoners, and he had talked about it and written about it incessantly. "I've pushed it out of my mind. I've blocked out the worst scenes, except for a few that I've been unable to forget: a man whose head was smashed in because he was found in the barracks during working hours, and the hangings we were forced to watch.

"At first I couldn't look. I didn't want to, but they made us look. Later I said to myself, 'You *must* watch, so you'll be able to take revenge.' Sometimes when the Russians were hanged, they'd sing the *Partizana* or shout out Stalin's name. We'd be ordered to remove our caps: '*Mützen ab.*' And then Dr. Thilo, one of the SS doctors, would give the signal, the trapdoor would swing open, and that'd be the end of that. It's strange, really. I saw hundreds of people die every day, but I remember a scene like that down to the last detail."

"All those corpses," Yehuda remarks. "That wasn't death, that was daily life. The dead *Muselmänner** whose bodies were carted off behind the barracks as though they were garbage – we hardly noticed anymore."

Dov's eyes seek refuge in the drawings on the wall, and I realize that we should move on quickly to another topic. He takes the initiative himself: "Religion helped some of the Orthodox kids in our group. Sinai A., who survived

* Literally "Muslims." Concentration-camp slang for the men who had lost the will to live.

and later became a rabbi, even tried to fast on the prescribed days. But others went through a religious crisis
and lost their faith completely."

Yehuda cuts in: "You had to hold onto something. In my
case it was the thought that I wanted to survive. It was a
deliberate decision. Because I wanted to take revenge, to
tell others. Determination, fueled by anger. Or perhaps it
was instinct. We reacted the way an animal would: one
false move, one wrong step, one finger accidentally
brushed against the barbed wire, one stolen potato found
in your possession, one unfortunate movement during a
selection, and you'd be killed. You couldn't let your guard
down, not even for a minute."

Yehuda and Dov exclaim, almost in chorus: "Once you
lost the will to live, you were done for."

I go back to an earlier point. "Those stripes in the sky
made by the American planes – they made me feel
hopeful too."

Not Yehuda. "I was afraid that they were German
planes, that they'd machine-gun us or drop a bomb on us
during roll call. I'd think, 'This is it, now they're going to
kill us.'"

Dov's face clouds over. "I felt both. Sometimes they
gave me a feeling of hope, but more often one of despair."

Our conversation likewise appears to be jumping back
and forth between darkness and light. I'm relieved when
Yehuda veers off on another tangent: "To deal with my
fear, I dreamed up all kinds of fantasies. I heard somebody talking about Spinoza, and in my childish brain, I
made a mishmash of philosophical ideas about the immor-
tality of the soul. I drew circles in the sand to represent

transcendental spheres – whatever those were – and thought to myself, 'We're all immortal, eternal.'"

This evokes a precious memory, which I share with Dov and Yehuda. After the selections, I lost track of Peter, one of the older boys. Peter used to recite fragments from Schiller's *Räuber* that he remembered from school. He hoarded them like a treasure because they represented something from his past life at home, something he could cling to. But also because they were about justice. Our whispered conversations about Schiller were moments of happiness for me.

Dov adds eagerly: "When I was in the infirmary, I lay next to a dying *Muselmann* named Herbert. He talked about things I'd never heard of before and gave me a book that I read later when I was back in the Men's Camp. Dostoyevsky's *Crime and Punishment*. I had no trouble imagining Raskolnikov's anguish and remorse after he'd killed the old woman. It had nothing to do with the wholesale slaughter going on around me. My memory of the outside world was rather vague, but my sense of justice was still intact, and one simple murder was abhorrent to me. My conscience extended not only to our group, but much further . . . thanks, perhaps, to Dostoyevsky."

This touching story reduces me to silence. Yehuda, too, has to swallow hard a few times. Then he remarks that the children from the Polish ghettos were a lot tougher because they'd lived amid death and destruction since 1939 and had been exposed to hunger, cold, filth, and neglect for three or four years more than we had.

Like a pendulum, our conversation swings back to the fact that the experience we'd picked up in the camps had helped us during selections. We knew that you had to hold in your stomach to make your chest look bigger. That, if asked, you should say you knew a trade. That your age had to fall within the limits currently considered safe.

Yehuda and I know that Dov's life was hanging on a thread in July 1944 and he knows that we know. Still, he can't resist the urge to relate that harrowing episode: "Schwarzhuber wanted to send me back because I was under thirteen and was too small. So I got in line again. The second time I lied, and I made it through all right!" There's a note of triumph in his voice. He pauses to reflect, then continues: "I acted purely on instinct. The thought of annihilation hadn't really penetrated to my brain. I was like an animal fighting for its life. My psyche had rejected reality. That's what happens when you find yourself in a situation that seems totally hopeless. I know it sounds ridiculous, but your hopes and dreams don't get shattered."

I hear the sound of children's voices in the living room next door. Yehuda's wife Lea is trying to hush them, but isn't having much success. Yehuda, who'd been on the verge of saying something, drums his fingers in irritation, then stands up and reluctantly leaves the room, as if in a trance. Dov and I look at each other like two sleepwalkers who've just been awakened. We're in the process of turning our cassettes over when Yehuda hurries back in. Pointing to the tape recorders, he says, "Don't switch them off. I've just remembered a couple of things that were important to our group." He sits down, and within seconds we're plunged back into the theme of survival as though there's never been an interruption.

"Most of the prisoners never left their section of the

camp or even their own barracks except early in the morning to go to work or roll call. Their freedom of movement was more limited than ours. We were part of the *Rollwagenkommando*, the Cart Squad, and we dragged and pushed that thing all over Birkenau. We didn't feel as cooped up as they did, didn't numb ourselves to reality quite as fast. Our horizon was broader, and maybe that allowed us to distance ourselves more."

"That was also true of the metalworkers," interjects Dov. "And the skilled laborers and the errand boys."

"But," Yehuda says softly, with a tinge of shame, "we thought we were a cut above the other prisoners. Mainly because until August '44 most of us still had a full head of hair. But also because we had been housed in the 'punishment block.' The SS hated coming there – the Russians and Poles scared them to death, and their status rubbed off on us. Besides that, some of the older prisoners treated us well because they'd lost their own children. Stein, for example, the kapo of the *Rollwagenkommando*, used to rant and rave whenever the SS was around and pretend to beat us really hard. But he held himself in so he wouldn't inflict any real damage, even though he knew he might have to pay for it with his life. Every once in a while an SS man would appoint one of the boys to be a work foreman. But that wasn't the same as the relationship between kapos and prisoners."

His last sentence fills me with doubt. I remember – with all too vivid clarity – a scene in which one of those quasi-kapos from our group mercilessly beat another boy to a bloody pulp. I spare Yehuda this memory. Why should I rob him of his illusion of camaraderie? I try to hide my skepticism, but don't know if I'm having any success. To my relief, Lea calls Yehuda to the phone.

After his return, we dare to admit that we're feeling drained and tired. Still, we aren't ready to stop. There's so little time.

Yehuda speaks faster, as if to make use of every minute. "Gerhard should send questionnaires to all of the 'boys' in our group who survived the war. Explain what we've talked about today and prod their memories. In other words, he should become our chronicler."

Dov reels off a number of items he feels are a must: the role of fantasy and reality, our present philosophies, our fears, surviving in a small group, in a mass, or alone, maintaining moral values, our political views. He's so tired his stream of words begins to slow to a trickle.

But Yehuda bounces back like a boxer after the bell. "We need to make sure politicians don't exploit the Shoah. A while ago a couple of filmmakers were working on a documentary about one of our great statesmen, and they wanted me to say I survived the camps because of my traditional, warm, Jewish background. That really galls me. If a politician or anyone else wants to learn from our experiences – assuming anything can be learned – they should listen to what we have to say rather than using us to justify their actions."

Dov, speaking with emotion, adds: "My past hasn't inured me to cruelty. During the various wars Israel's had to fight, I saw numerous acts of cruelty, and I was upset by every one of them. What really depresses me are the diehards in the government and the Knesset, almost none of whom have had any personal experience of the Shoah, who are always screaming bloody murder. Of course those of us who have been through it react in many different ways. Some shut their minds to metaphysical questions, just wanting to lead a quiet existence, happy to be alive, trying to find safety and security. Like me, they wear a mask to hide their deepest fears."

Our orderly conversation is starting to come unraveled. I want to interrupt, to share my theory that there's no such thing as one kind of survivor. That our view of what's happened depends on our personalities, talents, physical condition, past and present circumstances, images of then and now, chance encounters, etc.

But before I can begin, Yehuda exclaims, his face filled with despair, "I don't think in political terms, and I'm not the type to wear a mask!"

"You have the good fortune to be an artist," I reply.

"That helps," he says, "but I don't have both feet firmly planted on the ground. It's so hard just to live an everyday life. I often say to myself, 'How can you take yourself seriously, how can you take the world seriously – you, a man who was in Auschwitz?'

"At a PTA meeting, everybody gets excited about something, all puffed up with self-importance, and I think, 'Why all the fuss?' At the funeral of a dignitary I think, 'One man? Important? What's important?'

"When I arrived in the camp, I was the age my children are now. Can I understand their problems, their worries? Not really. The 'boys' from our group that I write to are wrestling with the same things. Regardless of their professions. The mask doesn't suit any of us very well."

Yehuda continues thinking out loud. "I often write in my diary," he says, speaking more to himself than to us, "that I'm depressed, that I suffer from the world just like

Paul Celan and Jean Améry. They didn't see a way out. But my work helps me get over my depressions. I don't know what sets them off. Auschwitz? Worry? Hypersensitivity? And to think that after the war I was lucky enough to wind up in an orphanage with a man like H. G. Adler looking out for my education and welfare."

After a moment of introspection, Dov adds: "It's hard to know where our depressions come from. I usually get over mine fairly quickly. One time it took a lot longer. I'd gone to Warsaw for a conference. A fellow historian who was working there took me on an excursion to Lodz, Gdansk, and Auschwitz. On the way there he said: 'As long as we're going to Auschwitz, you really ought to see Birkenau – that was the actual death camp.' If he'd asked me if I'd been a prisoner there, I think I'd have said yes. But he didn't ask, and I didn't tell him. I couldn't remove the mask. He still doesn't know. A taxi brought me to Birkenau and back. I thought seeing it might help me get over my nightmares. It didn't."

The sound of children's voices next door brings us back to the present. Lea makes no attempt to quiet them, and I'm glad. We're exhausted, ashen, unable to go on. Dov and I silently put away our tape recorders, while Yehuda throws open the window of his studio. The sun is still shining. There's a gush of fresh air. A dog barks, and the notes of Mozart's Prague Symphony float in from a distance. Yehuda grins: *"Na! . . . Kinder, weitermachen!"*

That lighthearted "Okay, kids!" combined with the old SS command to "carry on" is so absurd that Dov and I burst out laughing. What would we do without humor, I think to myself.

Like a bunch of guilty schoolboys who've played longer than they were supposed to, we say good-bye. Yehuda, visibly moved, stands in front of his house and waves until the car disappears from view.

The candle of my time in Israel was now burning at a rapid rate. I spent the last days frantically going through Dov's Oral History archives. I phoned my newly acquired "brothers," bid farewell to old friends and new, took some long-overdue notes, and walked around the golden walls of the Old City one last time to imprint the centuries-old, timeless scene on my brain forever.

I packed my bags in the cool early-morning hours of a Friday, trying to distribute the piles of paper, books, and tapes so that the hinges of my suitcase wouldn't break. My solicitous landlady, afraid I might starve to death on the way home, prepared one last copious meal and urged me to rest before my long journey.

She gently closed the front door behind her. The midday heat beat mercilessly down outside. The blinds in my room projected a striped prison uniform on the wallpaper. I dozed off. My dream turned into a nightmare. The roll-call bell rang once, twice. The third ring brought me back to my room in Jerusalem. Half-asleep, I stumbled to the door, sure that my landlady had forgotten her key.

I opened the door. A short man in a long black coat was standing in the doorway, framed by blinding sunlight. His chest was covered with a gray beard. He had on a black hat and a pair of round wire-rim glasses. In his left hand he was clutching a book with a yellow jacket, and in his right a large white handkerchief, which he used to mop his brow. Shyly, he asked in flawless German what my name was, addressing me formally as *"Sie."* I supplied the requested information. His eyes, magnified by the thick lenses, were rimmed with red, presumably the glare of the sun. Or were those tears? He looked at me in silence for a long moment, then said in a kind of whisper, as if he didn't want to jolt me out of my sleep: "I'm Sinai A. Yehuda called and told me you were here. I hope I'm not disturbing you."

I never would have guessed that this small, unassuming rabbi was the Orthodox boy I'd known in the camp. His bashfulness made me bashful as well. I asked him in, cleared off a chair, and motioned for him to sit down. No, he didn't want a soda or anything else. A glass of water would be fine.

"I brought you something," he said. "A book about us and how we were saved by the Holy One, blessed be He."

I recognized the drawing on the yellow cover: one of Yehuda's. I couldn't read the Hebrew text or Sinai's dedication on the flyleaf.

We hesitantly exchanged a few words. There were long pauses. Our worlds were too far apart, and yet there was an old bond. He left after less than an hour, apologizing because it was soon going to be Shabbat and he had duties to attend to. I watched him go with a mixture of affection and doubt. The book about us and "how we were saved by the Holy One, blessed be He" weighed heavily in my hand.

Why us and not the others?

DINNER AND CONVERSATION IN QUEENS

An endless line snaked its way to a series of yellow
cubicles. Impassive American immigration officials
leafed through passports, snapped out questions, and
stamped visas issued in faraway lands. Thick red cords
meandered in and out until they reached a gleaming
stripe, where female attendants in trim uniforms regu-
lated the flow of passengers. The new arrivals waited
between the ropes, advancing slowly, one step at a time.
Some were impatient, others resigned. The serpentine
line kept growing. A couple of kids turned the ropes
into hurdles and jumped back and forth between
the rows, but no one else dared step across those
scarlet barriers. American officialdom apparently had
a calming effect on tempers that would have exploded
elsewhere.

Here, in the stifling entryway to the New World, I was
mesmerized by the multiethnic murmurs of the crowd
and the whine of the inadequate air conditioning. The
scene before me conjured up images from a distant past.
Long lines of men and women waiting in front of soup
kettles and bread rations, water taps and latrines, tattooers
and clerks. The impotent rage - coupled with fear and

impatience – that burned in me then still smoldered in me now.

The immigration officer stamped my passport without a word, seeming to stare right past me with watery blue eyes. Cheeks shaved to a silky sheen, stony face as motionless as a sphinx. The mask didn't drop an inch, not even for the beautiful Indian woman in an exotic sari who was next in line.

I waited for my luggage in JFK's chaotic baggage-claim area. At the far end of the room customs officials were standing behind low counters, inspecting the bags of the passengers who'd already plucked their worldly belongings from the carousel. I peered anxiously at the procession of tumbling and bumping bags, but my luggage was nowhere in sight. A wave of pessimism washed over me. I was sure that my tape recorders, embedded in the socks and shirts in my suitcase, had been either lost or damaged. How would I ever be able to remember the stories of my fellow camp inmates without them? After fifteen minutes that seemed like an hour, I saw a familiar set of bags heading my way – undented, undamaged.

I obediently waited my turn behind a noisy family with a cluster of children. According to the tags, they were from Islamabad. While the father untied various oilcloth bundles, two of the customs inspectors rummaged around suspiciously in the rest of their baggage. This went on for several very long minutes. Finally, one of them turned to me, leaving the other to grope for contraband, and asked me a standard question about whether I'd brought in anything besides clothing. I dutifully reported my tape recorders. His boyish face clouded over. He

frowned and demanded to see the contents of my suitcase. What was the purpose of my visit to the United
States? Where was I staying? How long was I going to be
here? Who was I planning to meet?

The unexpected interrogation surprised, annoyed, and
upset me. How could I possibly explain to this young
blond whippersnapper what I hoped to accomplish and
whom I expected to talk to? Keeping my words to a
minimum, I told him I'd come to see some people I used
to know in the camp. "What camp?" he asked. I said the
name I hate to say out loud. His eyes opened wide, then
quickly looked away. He carefully closed my suitcase, set it
down gently in front of me, and, in an almost inaudible
mutter, wished me luck during my stay in New York.

`I let the tide of passengers carry me along to the exit.
After the excitement of the trip, the arrival formalities,
and the baggage check, a kind of passivity, a mild fatalism,
took hold of me. I didn't dare think of what would happen
if my friend Dick didn't show up and I had to find my
way to my first address on this unknown continent all by
myself. Would I recognize him – an American who'd gone
to medical school in Holland and had returned to the US
with his family thirty years ago? Would he recognize gray,
bearded, balding me? Would we find each other in this
babel of gesticulating, shouting, and waving people?

Outside the terminal I blinked at the glaring sun,
shining down on the recently disembarked passengers
like a spotlight. Hundreds of people were crowded
around the exit. Their eyes glided over everyone who
emerged from the terminal, and I tried to pick out a face I
hadn't seen for half a human lifetime. A male voice called
my name, pronouncing it in a mixture of Dutch and

English. My eyes searched and found him almost immediately. A male arm waved. I waved back. His face still had the same friendly catcher-in-the-rye features I remembered. We gave each other a bear hug, clapped each other on the shoulder, and repeated each other's name. The intervening years melted away. We might be graying and overweight, bespectacled and wrinkled, but we were still the same twenty-year-olds we were in the 1950s.

Dick drove down the twelve-lane highway to Long Island in a sea of cars, all cruising at steady speeds in highly disciplined rows. Before I even had time to ask about his family, he said in a low voice, "Amy and I are divorced." He stared straight ahead, awaiting my reaction, my opinion.

For several minutes I was speechless. Moments of happiness flashed through my mind like a series of snapshots. The young Jewish American medical student and his charming, smiling wife . . . their son Michael whose first word was "van Gogh" . . . their sunny, modern home in one of Utrecht's new suburbs, with a secondhand Skoda parked out front . . . Dick's father, the ideal family doctor, full of Yiddish humor, heartbroken every time he had to take leave of his loved ones . . . Dick's overweight, over-anxious, interfering mother, who ordered her son and daughter-in-law around as if they were still teenagers . . . Dick and Amy's friends and fellow students, seated in the living room with generously filled glasses in their hands, discussing every topic under the sun except their studies, since most of them had spent the better part of the evening in their garrets poring over their books . . . Amy teaching her laughing child to walk . . . Dick tossing him in the air . . . Michael sitting on my lap . . . both Dick and

Amy listening with compassion to my stories of the war that nobody else wanted to hear, providing wordless comfort.

My silence prompted the confession that Dick was eager to make. Bashful at first, his words dripped like a leaky faucet and gradually swelled to a stream: short sentences full of resignation and justification. I gathered that during his residency – years of penny-pinching economy, long-term loans, eighty-hour work weeks, and growing children – Amy's and Dick's once happy marriage had steadily eroded. A wall of alienation had been erected between them. And the two mothers-in-law, both possessive Yiddish mamas, had helped cement each brick. The death of his father – the kindly doctor whose mild humor had reconciled them on more than one occasion – had only hastened their estrangement.

Dick had became a surgeon on Long Island. In the same town where he'd been born, where his father had been an outstanding GP, where he'd done his residency, where everyone had known him since he was a little boy . . . and where his marriage had slowly run aground. Amy turned to the outside world. She went back to school, got a degree, and started working part-time in a crisis center for Puerto Ricans. Amy had liberated herself. From housewife to professional social worker in the space of a few years.

The traffic thinned out the further we got from the city. Blue road signs bearing Indian place-names spanned the freeway. Tense, Dick kept his eyes on the road, avoiding my eyes. "I married Joan four years ago. She was my OR nurse. She still is. She's looking forward to meeting you. She's curious, but also a little nervous. We met at the hospital about seven years ago. In the beginning the children didn't want to have anything to do with her. Amy didn't either, not even after the divorce. She sees Joan as an intruder, the non-Jewish outsider, the shiksa. In the meantime the boys have gotten used to her. My daughter Lisa is only a few years younger than Joan, and she now accepts her as a friend. Amy is still living in the big house. We talk to each other fairly often. I called and told her you were coming. She'd really like to see you, and she hopes you can come and stay with her for a few days."

His words sounded flat, like he was dictating a medical report. In the ensuing silence I decided to keep my opinion to myself. I nodded without saying anything, outwardly understanding, but inwardly shocked.

By the time we exited the freeway at the blue Rockville Centre sign, the tension had ebbed away. Our former bond had apparently been restored. The main street of this small commuter town had the familiar look of every American city I'd ever seen in the movies. There was a long orderly strip of shops, pizza parlors, and supermarkets, mostly one story. Anything higher than that was a rarity. Here and there a parking lot stood out like a gaping hole between two jagged teeth. Garish signs attempted to lure customers to a motley collection of shops and grocery stores surrounded by abandoned shopping carts. The ugliness began to taper off only as we left the commercial zone. There was a modern post office, a white, quasi-rustic restaurant at the end of a tree-lined drive, and a Chase Manhattan bank with gold-tinted windows.

Dick made a right-hand turn and we entered another world: a chic residential neighborhood. Big, beautiful colonial-style houses with verandas and porticoes. Every so often a drab stone house would be overshadowed by the colorful shingled houses on either side. The painters had had an amazing palette to choose from – everything from dark blue to bright orange. The lawns in the lovingly tended gardens looked like they'd been clipped with nail scissors. A vacant house with peeling paint and knee-high grass stuck out like a sore thumb: a potential haunted house à la Chas Addams.

At the end of the street, half-hidden by tall firs, was a red clapboard house with a Dutch door and an overhang supported by white pillars in the George Washington tradition. Dick, a little nervous at the upcoming meeting between Joan and me, pointed to the house and said deprecatingly, "Well, this is it. Anyway, it's big enough for the two of us."

He led the way over a brick path that cut through a weedless carpet of grass, opened the door, and called into the silent house: "Honey, we're here . . ."

One look, and I felt like I'd landed in a Hollywood set. A dining room with a walnut table polished to a gleam. Beyond that a kitchen, from which a youthful blonde as trim as a teenager emerged. Dark eyes briefly looked me up and down. An almost imperceptible frown changed instantly into a friendly but fragile smile. She welcomed me rather formally, not daring to give me a kiss. She asked about the plane trip, my jet lag, my family, wondered whether I'd like to freshen up for dinner, and showed me to my room upstairs. The timeworn staircase, smelling of beeswax and burnished to a velvety shine, sighed at every step.

The guest room, with its spanking-new four-poster bed, glistening brass lamps, and spotless Grandma Moses armchairs once again made me feel I'd wound up on a movie lot. I changed clothes and creaked back down the stairs. Dick and Joan were waiting for me in a spacious living room furnished with a green L-shaped couch, easy chairs, and Swedish end tables with big brass ashtrays. Here, too, everything was immaculate and painfully neat. After a glass of bourbon, served in crystal tumblers, Joan announced with a hint of pride that we were going to have "a real American dinner." It was about as American as they come: meat loaf, corn on the cob, baked potatoes, fresh peas, and California wine, with apple pie and coffee for dessert.

The conversation drifted along on the surface: a postop patient of Dick's that needed to be called . . . Joan's work schedule for tomorrow . . . her evening classes . . . the discomforts of air travel . . . a vacation in Shakespearean England they'd both enjoyed so much in the spring. Not a word about Holland, not a word about the reason for my trip, though I'd mentioned it in my letter.

During dessert a Jewish friend of Dick's and Joan's appeared on the doorstep with his young, non-Jewish, second wife, who was introduced to me as "a real Bostonian." The two women retired to the kitchen, chatting away, and the men moved to the living room. Suddenly, with no warning, Hank put his hand on my shoulder and said in a low voice, as though he didn't want his words to carry to the kitchen: "Dick's told me all about you. I'm interested in your plans. Many of my father's relatives were killed in camps in Poland."

His abrupt openness startled me. Dick motioned for him to stop. Behind his bifocals Hank's cheerful, smiling eyes took on the stricken look of a chastised schoolboy. Just as I was on the point of asking my old friend Dick why he was avoiding the topic and had cut Hank off, the kitchen door swung open. The women came back in, apparently without a care in the world. All at once I realized that the two husbands preferred to let the unspeakable past remain unspoken in front of their young shiksa wives. Dick, ever the considerate host, asked everyone what they wanted to drink and led the conversation around to my children, my wife, Europe, Reagan. What were they afraid of? Did they think that suffering was catching, that you could be infected with *it*, with the Shoah, that you might pass it on? Were they leery of compassion? Were they afraid of being recognized as "the other," the unassimilated ghetto Jew? Of not being taken seriously in a gentile world, in which anti-Jewish sentiment can erupt at any moment?

My musings were interrupted by the departure of the newlyweds. They hadn't stayed long, and I couldn't avoid the impression that they'd failed to perform the role of buffer that had consciously or unconsciously been assigned to them. Was it mere courtesy that made Hank's wife remark as she was leaving that meeting me had been "very exciting"? Had there been more to that lighthearted small talk in the kitchen? My suspicions were confirmed when Joan sat down across from me, assumed a serious expression, and gently but firmly said, "Gerry, please tell me what your trip to the US is all about!"

Dick's shoulders slumped, his facial muscles relaxed. "I guess she might as well hear the whole story," he said, like someone caught in the act.

Tired from the journey and the six-hour time difference between the two continents, I was having trouble keeping my eyes open. But Joan's modest, heartfelt question chased away any ideas of sleep. I briefly sketched my life as a child in Nazi Germany, my boyhood in Holland, my camp years during the war, my return to Holland, my days as a college student in Utrecht where I'd met Dick and Amy, my years of work as a sociologist, and the moment when the past began to torment me both mentally and physically.

"Is that when you started to write?" she dared to interject. Her eyes hadn't left my face for a moment.

I explained what had prompted me. How I'd begun by poking around in archives. How I'd been motivated by wanting to find out more about survival, other survivors, the reason for the barbarism. I told her of my searches in London, Paris, Amsterdam, and Jerusalem. Of my surprise and joy when I discovered two of my former camp inmates in Israel, and how they knew of more survivors from the same transport. How we'd decided to record for posterity our lives before, during, and after the war. How I'd taken it upon myself to gather these testimonies, and how I'd come to the US and Canada in search of the stories of those who had shared my fate, our fate.

I stopped. The only sound was that of our breathing. Joan stared straight ahead and tried, not very successfully, to hide her emotions. Dick coughed and laid a hand on my arm. "Feel free to use our house as your home base for as long as you want. You can invite people here and make use of any facilities we have to offer. We'll try to make it easier for you in whatever way we can. We'd be proud to be of assistance," he said, almost formally. Joan nodded, glad to be of help, glad to be part of the undertaking.

Their enthusiasm caught me by surprise. I fended off their generosity, explaining that I couldn't stay more than a week because my friends were located in various parts of the US and Canada and that it was necessary for me to meet them in their own surroundings.

Pleased at the renewed friendship, I retired to my four-poster. My first night in the United States – restless and full of kaleidoscopic dreams – began for me at the hour in which most people in Holland were setting off for work.

Friday. I awoke to sunlight streaming through Venetian blinds. An unfamiliar bedroom, except for my suitcase and my clothes, flung over a chintz armchair. The mists of sleep began to clear. I was in America. On Long Island. At the house of friends. There was work to be done, lots of work, too much work. I was beset by doubts. Would I be able to handle it? Would I find the people I was looking for? Would they agree to see me?

The search had begun. But was I pointed in the right direction?

Still in my pajamas, I explored the empty house. Dick and Joan had left for the hospital two hours earlier. They'd laid out breakfast for me, but instead of sitting at the table I gobbled my food standing up. I felt strangely restive. Seated at Dick's desk, I realized that the month I had ahead of me was far too short.

Frustrating phone calls with secretaries, cleaning ladies, and children who didn't know what I was talking about. Unanswered rings from napping phones. " . . . The family is on vacation . . .", " . . . Mr. So-and-so is away on business . . .", " . . . They're in the Adirondacks for the weekend . . .", " . . . Professor Wiesel won't be back in the office till Monday . . .", " . . . May I take a message? . . ."

I don't know which I felt more: impatience, irritation, or fear of failure.

In a fatalistic mood, I called John F., a short, stout, high-strung accountant from Toronto who'd poured out his life story to me six months ago in an old-fashioned hotel room in Amsterdam. From the moment we'd noticed how our paths had crossed in Birkenau in 1944, all thoughts of the tape recorder on the table had vanished.

Johnny excitedly rattled off advice, dictated phone numbers and address changes of "the boys," as he called our group of survivors, and renewed his promise to help me in my search. He reported with pride that he'd located Ludek K., another one of the boys, whom we'd assumed was dead. In 1968 Ludek had managed to exchange the chilly aftermath of the Prague Spring for the warmth of a Canadian summer. He was in poor health, but free.

The push buttons kept beeping their monotonous melodies until a voice welcomed me from Edison, New Jersey. Harry G., up to that moment only a name on my list, invited me to come talk to him. At last, my first appointment in the New York area. But days later than my schedule allowed.

One name on my list didn't have a phone number. The street was somewhere in Queens, but I couldn't find it on my map. I rifled through the thick telephone directories, peering desperately at the numbers. I was out of luck. There was no one by that name. Perhaps it was a misprint. I impatiently called Information. I spelled the name, expecting to be told there was no listing. To my surprise, Karel P. did exist. My joy was quickly tempered by annoyance – he had an unlisted number. The operator was sorry, but she couldn't help me any further. Not one to be deterred, I dialed Customer Service. Having come all the way across the ocean, I wasn't about to give up so easily. I became entangled in a web of bureaucracy, but I hung in with the determination of a bulldog. At long last I was connected to a department that was prepared to call P. and ask him to contact me.

I went off to cool my phone fury under the shower. After a while I heard a piercing ring. A hoarse voice, loud and suspicious, barked "Who're you?" in an accent so thick I could hardly understand what he said.

I told him my name, adding that I was in New York and that I wanted to talk to him about the letter and questionnaire I'd sent him. This was greeted with a short silence.

"What letter?"

I explained my reason for coming to the US. He mumbled something to himself. Then, as if he were awaking from a dream, he said, "Oh, yeah, that letter. But I wasn't really part of your group."

"But your name is on Yehuda's list of survivors of Men's Camp B II D!"

He sighed audibly into the phone. "I arrived later than everyone else, and I had very little to do with your group."

I began to doubt the value of a visit. I could feel his resistance, his protective armor. I wondered how I could end this macabre conversation without hurting his feelings.

I heard a woman arguing in the background. He hurled a Czech curse into the room. Then, suddenly, he was calmer, his English clearer. "Can you come to my house on Monday? I'll meet you at 4:00 o'clock by the Queens Village station."

I was astonished. "Okay," I said.

"Good," he growled, and hung up.

I dutifully went on phoning, as if to overcome my stage fright. What had seemed hopeless at the beginning of the day was now moving along fine. My agenda was full: Bonnie in Brooklyn, Misha in Boston, Jindra in Buffalo, De Caspers in Syracuse, Hilberg in Burlington. The tide had turned, my journey hadn't been in vain. I now had two days of carefree relaxation ahead of me.

Saturday. Amy, pleased at my visit and surprised by the timelessness of old friendships, showed me around Long Island and took me to see her elderly mother, whose German accent hadn't worn off after fifty years in the US. The past evoked a combination of nostalgia and revulsion. To the mother it meant Berlin: the glitter of the 1920s, the flames of the 1930s. To the daughter it meant wedded bliss in the 1950s, bitterness in the 1960s.

She gave me a tour of the red-brick junior college where she taught sociology under the direction of somber nuns in white habits. On the surface she seemed very much in command, but her broken marriage had left undercurrents of insecurity.

Sunday. No obligations. I wanted to get a taste of the Big Apple, as advertising yuppies had so childishly dubbed New York. The highway to the Manhattan Bridge was like a gently undulating lake with hundreds of gently bobbing sea gulls. Once again, I was amazed at how calmly Americans drive their cars. As we went along, Dick pointed out buildings and places that reminded him of his childhood. Joan looked out the window without comment. Neither of them mentioned my day with Amy. The wounds were still fresh.

The landscape around us started turning to stone, with only occasional patches of green. The horizon was shrouded in a pale-blue mist through which you could see the vague contours of mountains. The drivers began to lose their self-discipline, impatiently racing their engines like jockeys before the finish. The city was exerting its pull. Dick pointed through the windshield at the mist clearing in the distance. Those weren't mountains, but the silhouettes of skyscrapers. I gasped. New York had shed its mask. Ever since my childhood, I'd seen that skyline in so many ads and movies that the real thing suddenly seemed unreal. We crossed the Manhattan Bridge and entered the city's scraggly outskirts: Chinatown. Behind the Chinese signboards and disorderly rows of houses, concrete and brick colossuses rose up into the sky. The pride of the metropolis, the symbol of the nation.

Speechless, I looked around me like a child at its first fair. I tried to catch a glimpse of the sky between the tall buildings. What had seemed overpowering ten minutes ago now seemed perfectly normal. Grand became grandeur. Cacophony in stone became an urban melody. Peering through the car windows, I underwent an enchantment. Manhattan: a sunlit grid of streets and avenues. Mind-boggling wealth and glittering luxury alongside squalid poverty and disgraceful decay. Romantic nostalgia next to kitschy futurism. Quality beside quantity.

Dick stopped the car in front of the Museum of Modern Art's dark glass facade. Majestic West 53rd Street was deserted. A red bicycle chained to a lamp post reminded me of the bikes outside Amsterdam's Central Station.

Like other visitors from the Old World, I felt overwhelmed by the mass of high-quality art. The paintings,
having obeyed the siren call of the mighty dollar, were
being pampered with light and space. Works I'd known
only from slides and reproductions could now be viewed
in their full glory. But for once I didn't feel the usual stir of
aesthetic excitement. My conscience was bothering me: I
was here on business. So I dutifully trotted off to another
wing of the museum to see an exhibit on Vienna before
the Anschluss: the *Welt von Gestern*, the World of Yesterday. In other words the world before the barbarism.
The world of Freud and Musil, of Zweig and Rilke, of
Wittgenstein and the Vienna Circle, of Klimt and Schiele,
of Bruno Walter and countless other great and hopeful
innovators. It was also the world that had been inhabited
by many of my friends, relatives, and fellow prisoners. The
world of the Austro-Hungarian Empire. A world in which
the names Theresienstadt and Mauthausen were associated with nothing more horrifying than narrow-minded
provincialism. A world in which the nobility was van-
ishing, but the arts and sciences were flourishing, despite
the oppression.

Monday. America in work clothes. On the platform of the
strictly utilitarian Rockville Centre station, men in well-
cut summer suits scan the morning news or read their
paperbacks with their black attaché cases resting beside
their shiny shoes. They only look up long enough to greet
their fellow commuters with a nod or a mumbled hello
before going back to their books. A few well-groomed
women in sweaters or linen suits are sitting on concrete
benches, clutching Big Brown Bags or briefcases and

impatiently scanning the tracks. Young people in jeans
are few and far between. A couple of students who've
overslept are talking to each other in loud voices. A long
stainless-steel train whooshes past and comes to a stop
only when the last car is also under the overhang. The
sluggish crowd is galvanized into action, with everyone
squeezing through the automatic doors as if there's not a
second to lose. Once inside, they continue to read or talk,
regardless of whether they're sitting down or standing up.

Almost no one is looking out of the windows. We glide
past brick office towers with opaque windows and past
vast construction sites, where the workers, crawling over
the concrete and steel frames, look like helmeted ants. A
nasal computer voice announces from a loudspeaker in
the ceiling: "Next stop, Jamaica Junction." The outside
world is not that of commuters, but of dust, noise, and
poverty. Of tenements, dirty hands, and sweat-stained
shirts. Only a few people get off, and like me they fan out
over the platforms to wait for other trains. The station is
old and drafty. The wrought-iron pillars supporting the
roof have been covered with endless layers of paint, and
the floors have been repeatedly patched: the kind of
genteel poverty that reminds me of the Depression, now
more than half a century ago.

The rattling train I board next cuts through a cityscape
of dreary little houses with tiny yards. Some of them are
neatly cared for, but most are filled with rusty refrigerators
and washing machines. Small factories and squat school
buildings appear to have been plunked down at random
in the middle of a residential area. The train comes to a
stop. Outside my window I see a battered sign: Queens
Village. It doesn't look like a station, and I hesitate to get

out. But then the name is called, and I take the plunge. The other passengers head for a run-down building with no doors at the end of the crumbling platform and disappear from view. Every window is smashed, every tile is broken. The stairwell reeks of urine, and there are several turds near the exit. No railway personnel, not even a ticket machine. Outside, the sun beats down on the dusty park where Karel P. is supposed to pick me up.

I sit and wait on one of the rickety benches. The weed-choked path is littered with beer cans, Coke cans, bits of paper, plastic throwaways. In back of me, people are cruising past the derelict station or trying to park their rusty, dented, oversized American cars. The steady beat of rock music booms through the windows. The majority of the drivers are black, their clothes shabby or bright. In front of me, cars and trucks rumble over a busy thoroughfare. Women with shopping carts are loading up on groceries in uninviting supermarkets. Everybody seems to be in a hurry. Everybody, that is, except the guys in the noisemobiles and a bunch of kids sitting or leaning against a park wall with a ghettoblaster turned up to full volume: blacks and whites united by alcohol and drugs. Two of them stagger to their feet and start hustling passersby, who quicken their steps and pretend they don't see them. There's not a policeman in sight, though a squad car occasionally races past. Half an hour later, I'm still waiting for Karel P.

All alone on my bench, in full view of that unsavory gang, I feel a sense of foreboding. I get up and walk over to another bench, occupied by a gray-headed black man and his grandson. He doesn't return my greeting. Distrust smolders under his eyebrows. As soon as I sit down, he gets up, as if to demonstrate that I shouldn't expect any protection from him.

I avoid eye contact with the group, but I can feel their glances. I know I should leave, but I'm afraid of missing P. Indecision keeps me rooted to the spot until two of the gang come slowly and menacingly towards me. The others watch as if it's feeding time in the zoo. The white kid, so drunk he can hardly stand, stops about twenty yards away from me. He raises his beer can and slurs, "Have a drink." His black pal, likewise reeling, laughs like a hyena. Their friends by the wall cheer them on. I stand up and walk calmly towards the street, trying to create the impression that their aggression has gone unnoticed. When the beer can lands beside me in a comet of foam, I decide it's time to pick up my pace. Panting, I reach a phone booth on the other side of the street. Only after dialing P.'s number do I check the whereabouts of my assailants. They haven't followed me: I'm nothing more to them than a momentary diversion in an ocean of gnawing boredom.

Karel P. sounds confused. Unwilling to admit he forgot our appointment, he tries to cover it up by saying he wasn't sure of the train schedule. But he promises to pick me up right away. We agree to meet at the store by the phone booth, since there's no way I'm going back to the park. A steady stream of cars and trucks whiz by. Every time I see a Chevrolet I think it's P., but so far I've been wrong. Then a black car zooms by, screeches to a halt, backs up, and stops in front of me. The passenger door swings open, and a hoarse voice with an unmistakably Czech accent orders me to get in fast and shut the door.

This isn't exactly how I expected former concentration-camp inmates to greet each other. He addresses me as Dr. Durlacher, while I call him Karel. Despite his many years in the New World, he's apparently been unable to shake his Central European titlemania. Since his eyes are glued on the road, all I can see is his profile. A round head with thinning hair, a snubby Socrates-like nose, and the purplish complexion of a person with high blood pressure. He's holding the steering wheel so hard his knuckles have turned white. Once we leave the busy traffic and enter the quieter residential district, his hands relax their grip and he stops muttering to himself. I ask him whether he has a wife and children, and he replies coldly that I would be seeing *her* in a few minutes and that he rarely has any contact with his daughter, who's married and lives in England with her husband and two kids. He starts to add "Thank God," but catches himself just in time.

The streets of his neighborhood look friendlier and neater than I'd suspected when I'd seen them from the train. Clapboard and shingled houses with small, well-tended lawns, colorful flower beds and garden statues in every conceivable shape and size. The car lurches to a halt in front of one of the houses. In the middle of the lawn is a sentimental pink and blue statue of the Virgin Mary. P. opens the gate and leads the way. I notice that he's short and stocky, not much taller than the statue. I can't help thinking that he's a walking time bomb.

Behind the front door, which is blocked from view by a screen, a dog is barking itself into a frenzy. P. opens the door and snarls a few words in Czech at the Schnauzer. "It's hers. He drives me crazy," he says half-apologetically, without looking at me. The backyard is lined with tall shrubs. In the shade of a laburnum, a woman in a housecoat is stretched out on a chaise longue, apparently deep in sleep. P. crosses over to her and says in an unnecessarily loud voice: "Dr. Durlacher is here, Jeanette." She doesn't wake with a start, but simply opens her eyes and looks at me. Smiling vaguely, she holds out her arm with theatrical elegance, as though she expects me to kiss her hand. The rouge on her cheeks does little to camouflage her paleness. Lipstick has been smeared over her small mouth in an attempt to make it seem bigger. She blinks constantly. Without saying hello, she apologizes for her housecoat, adding that she's only recently been discharged from the hospital. She still feels a bit weak.

"It wasn't a hospital, it was a psychiatric ward," P. bursts out. Jeanette continues to smile, but her narrow lips get even narrower. She sits up, looks at me: "He'd be better off if he got some help too." She rises languidly to her feet and brings us a pot of tea, which she'd apparently made while P. was picking me up. I sit in a lawn chair beside her and drink my tea from a Limoges cup while P. goes in to use the phone. She speaks hurriedly, as if she wants to give me a rundown of her entire life in the short time he's away. Nostalgia for France and Brittany, where she was born . . . the difficult years when she was first here . . . her work at an insurance company that provides a welcome addition to their shrunken income . . . a veiled reference to marital problems. When P. comes back with the dog, which he'd taken out for a walk after his phone call, Jeanette stops mid-sentence. Her eyelids, which had calmed down, start fluttering again. I feel sad and helpless.

When P. announces, in a voice that won't take no for an answer, that he wishes to talk to me privately in a

restaurant, I feel like canceling the interview. My biggest
fear is that he's going to explode with rage. I say good-bye
to Jeanette. Smiling listlessly, she disappears from my life.

During the drive to the restaurant, P.'s tension is almost
palpable. His wife's smile haunts me, but nothing makes
a dent in him. It's as if he's waiting impatiently at the
confessional so he can unburden himself of his memory.

We pull up at an unassuming restaurant, and he breaks
the silence. "I can talk here. It's a Czechoslovakian restaurant."

The owner is leaning over the bar chatting with a customer. He doesn't notice P. at first. A waiter comes over
and starts to lead us to a reserved table in the middle of
the room, but P. doesn't budge. In a loud voice, he says
something in Czech to the owner, who excuses himself to
his American guest, comes out from behind the bar, and
formally greets P. Although I get the gist of the conversation, P. repeats it in English for my benefit: "Professor
Durlacher has come over especially from Europe to interview me for a book he's writing, and we need a quiet
table." It's useless to argue. The owner ushers us through a
side door into a large, dimly lit dining area. The tables
have been set with white tablecloths, and a sideboard is
laden with wineglasses, dishes, hot plates, and silverware.
There's not a soul in sight. I feel a strong draft, and when
the lights are switched on, I notice gray curtains billowing
out from a set of French doors. The walls are covered with .
paintings of voluptuous nudes in old-fashioned drawing
rooms and hunting scenes. It's all I can do to keep from
laughing.

Even before we've settled into our plush armchairs,
Karel P. plunges into his story. "I knew Misha K. and Paul

K. when we were in the Men's Camp. They were put to work as errand boys for a *Blockältester* and a Polish officer, and they had enough to eat."

I'm so taken aback by this crude opening, blurted out in almost incomprehensible English, that I don't know what to say. In my confusion I press the wrong button on my cassette recorder, which is nestled among the china and the cutlery, and it refuses to start. P. wants to go on, but to my relief the waiter arrives to take our order. This gives me time to find my equilibrium again. I ask P. to tell me his story in chronological order. He gives me a dazed look, empties his beer glass in one swallow, beckons the waiter to bring him another, and begins to talk. This time he seems more hesitant, more precise, lost in thought. "I was born in December 1926, on Christmas Day. My parents had a mixed marriage – my father wasn't Jewish, but my mother was. Anyway, neither of them was religious. After they got married, my mother's family disowned her. As far as they were concerned, she didn't exist. That was the beginning of the tragedy.

"My father was a metalworker in a large factory near Prague. Then the Depression came, and the workers went on strike. He was one of the activists – he was on the strike committee. They lost. He was blacklisted and couldn't get a job anywhere. He couldn't support all five children, so the family was split up. My brothers were farmed out to other families. Then my mother got sick. When I was five I was adopted by a Christian family and baptized. But I couldn't adjust. I kept crying for my mother and wetting the bed. So they sent me back to my parents. My mother died soon after that, in 1932. My Jewish relatives turned up at her funeral and decided to take care of the children. I lived with them until Hitler came. They were deported and didn't survive. I was sent to work as a slave laborer. I was housed together with other half-Jewish boys. We worked in an SS storehouse, a former synagogue, where they kept things they'd stolen from the Jews."

He tells his story fairly mechanically, staring vacantly into space the whole time. The peace and quiet we'd been promised is an illusion, since the room has filled with chatting diners. Plates and glasses tinkle. Traffic sounds drift in through the curtains. P. apparently doesn't hear a thing. Not even the wailing sirens of police cars and ambulances. He barely notices the arrival of our dinner and another glass of beer. Suddenly, he turns to me and says, in the voice of a teacher addressing a pupil: "You'll like this. I met Eichmann there. He came to pick out a refrigerator. He spoke Hebrew to a young Polish Jew, that's why I remember him. He passed out cigarettes to a couple of the workers, though you could be deported if you were caught smoking."

We eat our meal, which has gotten cold, in silence. He wolfs down his food and continues in his monotonous singsong, though my plate is still half-full: "One day, in the summer of 1942, I had a bad toothache and went to Prague, to the dentist. I'd been given leave, but I forgot to sign out. The next day they threw me in jail because I hadn't shown up for work. They kept me locked up for a month. Then they sent me, under guard, to Theresienstadt. Just me, no other prisoners. Two of my brothers were already there, in one of the youth houses. Since I was the child of a mixed marriage, I was exempt from deportation until further notice."

He orders more beer. His face is red, and I ask him if he'd like to take a break. He vehemently shakes his head no. Then, as if he suddenly remembers something, he turns to me and asks if I knew Karl Löwenstein, the commandant of Theresienstadt's Jewish militia, the *Gettowache*. So anxious is he to tell his anecdote that he plunges in without waiting for my reply: "Löwenstein was an officer in the German army during World War I. He had a high rank, a chest full of medals, and the protection of several Wehrmacht officers, but he wound up in Theresienstadt anyway. Still, he was part of the prisoner 'elite.' He was put in charge of the *Gettowache*. He even talked SS Commandant Rahm into letting his men wear uniforms and carry clubs. Löwenstein was such a stickler that one time when he was allowed to join the SS for dinner, he pointed out that some of the officers had laid their revolvers on the table, which was a serious breach of military etiquette. I don't know how the SS reacted to his lecture. A couple of weeks later he asked the commandant and his staff to review a parade, the six-hundred men of the *Gettowache* that he'd drilled himself. He stood proudly at attention, next to Rahm. The top brass were obviously not as pleased as Löwenstein, because on October 28, 1944, the entire company of potential rebels was sent to Auschwitz. Along with many others who thought their 'exemptions' had made them safe, including me."

He gazes reflectively into space and mumbles, "I should have said I was a gardener, but I was stupid enough to tell the truth, that I worked in the kitchen. They could easily replace a kitchen helper. Oh, by the way, I was one of the first to come back to Theresienstadt. Me and three other guys. That was in April 1945. They welcomed us and asked us all kinds of questions, but I was too sick to talk. I'd caught pneumonia, pleurisy, and typhoid fever during the death marches. I was nothing but skin and bones. There was a German Jew there who was married to an American, and he gave me some cognac from a package his wife had sent. He brought me to the infirmary, and Count Bernadotte ordered them to give me medical treatment. I still remember seeing Bernadotte walking around the hospital with a monocle."

He keeps talking to himself, nonstop. His face has become a stiff mask and has gone from red to purple. Whatever sense of chronology he once had is now gone. He keeps losing the thread of his story. I listen intently, trying to make connections, but I'm worried about taxing his strength anymore. There's no point in trying to slow him down: the world of yesterday has supplanted that of today. Still, I've heard enough fragments to form them into a pattern – the theme is all too familiar, and the variations all too agonizing.

I gathered that when he was in Theresienstadt he was given certain privileges as a "*Halbjude*," a half-Jew, and enough food to keep from starving. One day he read a letter with a Birkenau postmark. The writer had said that he had to work hard in a bakery and wear a uniform, but that he led a reasonable existence. Karel P. concluded that life in "the East" couldn't be as bad as everyone said. Like many in Theresienstadt, he didn't believe the atrocity stories told by the men in the slave-labor units, so he wasn't particularly scared by the thought of "the East." Consequently, in the first few hours after his arrival in Birkenau, he was fairly calm. The shouts of the kapos and

SS men, the clubs, the throbbing engines of the army trucks transporting old people and women with small children, the numbers being tattooed on people's arms, the electrified fence – none of these threw him into a panic. Only later did the reason for the smoking chimneys at the end of the railroad tracks begin to dawn on him. The extent of his own gullibility then hit him with full force. For days he couldn't swallow a bite. He fell ill, and during a selection went to stand by those who were sick. Just then he spotted one of his older brothers in the other line, the one for the "healthy," and sneaked over to him. It was someone to hold on to in the midst of appalling loneliness.

In Block 13 of Men's Camp B II D, the same barracks in which I'd been housed along with the eighty-eight other boys who'd survived Mengele's selection three months earlier, he met Misha K. and Paul K. By that time the rest of the group had either died, been dragged off to other camps, or been dispersed over Auschwitz-Birkenau like grains of sand. Misha, Paul, and he were put to work as "errand boys." A few days before his eighteenth birthday, he got a job as a bricklayer in Auschwitz I. Before long the freezing weather made it impossible to mix cement, so he was transferred to Budy, a slave-labor compound with food warehouses. Life there was much more bearable. Thanks to the oats, corn, and sugar beets he was able to steal from the stables, his physical condition improved.

In January 1945, when the Russian troops started closing in, every prisoner who could more or less walk was evacuated towards the West on foot or in open freight cars or farm carts. Karel P. was given a place on a buck-board beside a guard. After weeks of crisscrossing Poland

and Germany, in which thousands of his fellow prisoners either died of hunger, cold, or thirst or were shot to death, he reached Buchenwald. Up to then his "family tree" had continued to offer some protection. A ride in a closed freight car, a chunk of bread, a cup of hot water from the steam engine's boiler – these meant the difference between life and death. In the chaos of the crowded camp, he lost his privileges, but was luckily befriended by a couple of French political prisoners. After three weeks he was transported to Rehmsdorf. He was put to work in a refinery, where gasoline was being manufactured out of lignite. Several times a day the Allies dropped firebombs and high explosives on the factory in an attempt to disrupt and halt production. Panicked guards ran for shelter in tunnels dug in the sand. The casualty rate among the prisoners was high. Even the SS had many dead and wounded.

Hunger reigned in the camp. Even the POWs were starving. A black American GI begged him for food and tried to exchange a gold necklace for bread. After a heavy air raid, everybody was ordered to evacuate. Taking advantage of the chaos, one hundred and fifty prisoners escaped into the forest of the Ore Mountains, together with a couple of guards who had ignored the order of the SS officers to liquidate the prisoners.

In the city of Leitmeritz near Theresienstadt, a sick and emaciated Karel P. ran into three refugees who had likewise survived the death marches from Auschwitz. The four boys were so hungry and exhausted that they reported to the gate of the Theresienstadt ghetto. It was still in German hands, though under the protection of the Red Cross. Feverish from typhus and emotion, he watched from the window of the infirmary as the Russian liberators entered the camp on May 9, 1945.

Karel P. stops at this point and stares straight ahead with unseeing eyes. He doesn't seem to realize I'm there.

During the long silence, images of my own liberation flash through my head. A childish feeling of envy creeps over me. He was better off than I was . . . he had privileges . . . maybe his non-Jewish father is still alive . . . Ashamed, I cast off these thoughts, lay my hand on his arm, and break the silence: "And then?"

He snaps out of his trance. Speaking slowly and coherently, he concludes his story. "After the war I spent a year and a half in hospitals and sanatoriums recovering from tuberculosis. There were no visitors. I didn't know if my father was still alive. After I was released, I went to Prague to look for him. I found out where he lived. At first I didn't dare ring the doorbell, because I'd heard he'd remarried. But my brothers and my mother's Jewish relatives were all dead or missing, so I went ahead and rang. My new stepmother opened the door. I told her who I was and where I'd been. She kept me standing on the doorstep. She said she'd make me a cup of coffee and give me a slice of cake, but that I couldn't sleep in her house because she was afraid I might give her little boy TB. She added that my father wouldn't get home until late.

"I saw my father twenty years later, just before he died. I forgave him then for not coming to see me."

The dining-room noise seems to come from far away. I merge our two stories in my mind. My Prague in June 1945: the joy of liberation and the dream of brotherly love. His Prague in 1947: bleak loneliness and blatant selfishness.

During the Beneš regime, Karel P. tried to finish school. But when the Communists took over on February 25, 1948, he had to choose between opportunism and freedom. Any kind of pressure after the years of humili-ation had become unbearable to him. He dropped out rather than face the choice. His former camp buddies threw some work his way. He was barely making ends meet with an occasional bookkeeping job when he met a Jewish girl, born in Bulgaria and raised in Israel, who was working for the Jewish Agency in Prague. He went with her to Israel. They got married and hoped for a better future.

As if misfortune is the norm, Karel P. continues dis-passionately, his face a wooden mask: "I didn't find the peace of mind I was looking for. I started working for the Zim Line, a clerical job on the freighters and passenger ships. Our marriage couldn't take it, and we split up in 1954. We had a daughter, and she stayed with her mother. I sailed on the America-Israel Line until 1959. Then I decided to start a new life in the United States. I got a job in the accounting department of a bank, and that's where I met Jeanette. She's older than I am, and a devout Cath-olic. She was born in France, in Brittany. Her family insisted on a church wedding, even though I don't believe in God. My Jewish friends said I was crazy and turned their backs on me. Now *she's* the one who's crazy. She's been in and out of mental hospitals. I'm on disability and earn only a third of what I used to. Who knows if she'll ever be able to work again? I didn't get any reparation money from Germany. I suppose there was a cutoff date for applications?"

He looks at me questioningly, and when I confirm that it's too late he falls into a gloomy reverie. Then he abruptly stands up and imperiously beckons the waiter. When I offer to pay, he turns purple and growls that he's not a pauper.

In the car on the way to Jamaica Junction, he once again retreats into his cocoon. His face resumes its fierceness, and he swears at every traffic obstacle. Outside the station, he tries to pass a couple of kids on a bike, and when he can't get by he unleashes a flood of Czech curses at them. Astonished, they peer inside the car, not understanding what it had taken me several long hours to figure out.

Our farewell is brief, almost formal. Neither of us says "Till we meet again."

Darkness swept past the train windows.

I was traveling through a no-man's-land, somewhere between then and now, trying to free myself of the tentacles of the past.

Meeting Karel P. had undermined my self-confidence. Could I handle the confrontation with my own past? Questions whirled through my head. What did I feel for him? Sorrow? Repugnance? Had his camp experiences damaged him for life? Or did his anger and bitterness come from having been so heartlessly abandoned in his childhood?

One conclusion inevitably pushed its way to the fore: my search was going to be much more than a search for stories. I'd been hoping to find a few signs of friendship and solidarity, a few pinpoints of light in a dark past that would ease the burden of remembrance. P.'s words, his behavior, his story had revealed my motives and stripped me of my naivety. The cold of the past was still nipping at my heels. I was reminded of Yehuda, four years ago in Jerusalem, saying, "I suppose everyone looks back on his childhood as a lost paradise." Applied to P., these words lost all meaning.

It seemed to me now that paradisal solidarity was an illusion. The only thing that could exist in that inferno was fleeting friendship. When every step or every word could be fatal, when every day threatened to be your last, when survival put everything into a different perspective, loyalty and friendship were as brittle as ice. We relied on mutual support and help in trying to stay alive, and woe be unto those who forgot the rule of reciprocity: *do ut des*.

Remembering our cool good-bye, I was filled with remorse. I'd repaid anger and self-defence with coldness. My expectations had been at fault. Why should he feel a bond he hadn't felt back then? Had we sympathized with him and the privileges accorded him on the basis of his "Aryan" blood and straight nose? Had I forgotten that our killers had deliberately applied the technique of divide and rule, had deliberately created wolves among the wolves, because that too would hasten our destruction? Privilege and corruption had driven a wedge in the mass of prisoners, where violence and hate had been able to flourish. Satisfying to the Nazis but deadly to us.

The closer I got to my postwar friend Dick's house, the calmer I became. Soon I'd be sitting across from him and his gentle wife in their peaceful house, trying to summarize today's adventures, and Queens would seem light-years away. With a little luck, it would feel like the camp was on another planet.

Dick was waiting outside the station. "Hi, old friend," he said, and graciously opened the car door.

I gratefully slid inside.

DUAL LOYALTIES

"Sorry, mister," panted a dark-haired schoolboy who bumped into me while sprinting to catch up with a friend. He ran on, his black velvet yarmulke held in place by hairpins.

Dozens of kids came swarming down the steps of a large school building that was already in need of repair, though it wasn't old. The girls, in pairs or in groups, were talking a mile a minute. The boys were in a bigger rush, wilder: liberated from the classroom. All of them had schoolbags or stacks of books under their arms.

I stopped and looked. It was a familiar scene, and yet something was wrong, something was missing. It slowly dawned on me: there was no color. It was like watching a black and white movie. No faded jeans or checked bermudas, no bright shirts or jackets or baseball caps, no sexy skirts or logoed T-shirts, not a trace of lipstick or eye shadow. Only black and white, white and black, in endless variations.

It wasn't a school uniform that made them look alike, though the girls were all wearing white stockings and the boys yarmulkes. Most of the adult males walking down the street were also dressed in black. Black hats, black caftans, black trousers, black shoes, black hair – as if every thread and fiber was required to absorb the light of Orthodoxy. Although the women had a bit more leeway, they hardly needed a color chart. The one person I saw in colorful clothes was certainly not from around here. He probably wasn't even Jewish.

When I'd first stepped out of Brooklyn's Avenue J subway station, this area had seemed like another ordinary, rather run-down neighborhood in New York's endless sea of houses. I'd had to transfer several times, and I was already late for my appointment at the Center for Holocaust Studies. High up on the elevated platform, I'd looked down at the usual patchwork of dusty supermarkets and aging Fords and Chevrolets.

The south side of the station had reminded me of Jerusalem's shopping streets. Men in rolled-up shirtsleeves and yarmulkes were lounging beside their displays, chatting with each other and with their customers – a colorful reflection of the world's population. Their hands were moving constantly to emphasize the loud flow of words.

An iron-girdered walkway stretching across the road brought pedestrians to the north side. Peering into the distance, I'd tried to pick out the Center, but hadn't seen any likely candidates. The walkway separated the two branches of Judaism as effectively as an international demarcation line: the flexible moderates in back of me, the unbending Hasidim in front of me, my destination somewhere in between.

On the cracked sidewalk below, I'd pretended I was back in the world of Isaac Bashevis Singer. The collision with the young yeshiva student had made me realize that Singer's world is still very much alive.

Across the street from the school was a nineteenth-century brick building with most of the paint worn off its tall windows. A security camera mounted above the doorway moved slowly from side to side.

There was no number. No nameplate. No sign of anyone inside. It didn't look like it could be the Center, and I wasn't anxious to climb the ancient stoop.

I walked down the street until I reached a school-like building with Hebrew letters over the entrance. I tried to spell them out, but failed miserably. Ashamed, I asked an Orthodox passerby whether it was the Center for Holocaust Studies.

Not a word passed his lips. He shook his head, making his earlocks dance, and pointed an outstretched arm at the building I'd just come from. He cast me a doubtful look, apparently unable to believe I might have any business there. Then he went on his way, shaking his head and muttering to himself, as if to say it was no place for an unbeliever. I retraced my steps and stood shyly before the door. When I rang the bell, the all-seeing eye zeroed in on me.

A young woman in modest dress, her hair gathered into a tight bun like the schoolteachers of my youth, cautiously opened the door with a friendly but expectant smile. Who did I wish to see? Did I have an appointment? I mentioned the name of Bonnie G. and held up my letter of invitation, and she was suddenly overflowing with helpfulness and enthusiasm. A guest from Holland, a survivor, a researcher!

In the tiny cloakroom, she told me in rapid, flawless English that Bonnie, the archivist, would be with me in a moment and that the head of the Center, Professor Yaffa

Eliach, was sorry to miss me, but that she'd been called away on business. "Why don't you have a look around while you're waiting for Bonnie?" she said as she opened the door to a large, high-ceilinged room. She crossed over to her typewriter and said something in Yiddish to the three gray-haired secretaries, who glanced up from their work with hardly a flicker of interest, while I stood rooted to the threshold, unable to say a word, much less utter a polite hello.

All four walls were plastered with huge blowups of photographs. Emaciated, hollow-eyed prisoners in striped tunics were staring at me from every corner of the room. Some with bony, shaved skulls, others with rumpled berets. One group digging ditches, backs bent, shovels clutched in skeletal, dirt-caked hands. Another being marched like marionettes past exacting SS guards. A well-fed kapo kicking a prisoner out of a barracks. An old man sprawled on the barbed wire, his face a gruesome death mask. The black wall in Auschwitz I, where executions were carried out. A selection of new arrivals in Birkenau, with a crematorium in the background. Piles of glasses, stacks of human hair, mounds of suitcases with the neatly lettered names and addresses of places now inhabited by others.

Horrified, I looked and tried not to see. Four years ago in Yad Vashem I'd scurried past pictures just like these. And to think that these women, whose parents, aunts, and uncles had gone up in the flames, sat here all day long, typing the reports of those who, like me, had tossed the dice in the game of life and death and won.

"Go ahead, look around," the young woman repeated with an encouraging nod, as though I were a customer in a chic modern-art gallery. Except that the display cases in this room were filled with camp relics instead of art.

They struck me as a desecration. How familiar and yet how menacing they were – the crudely carved wooden spoons, the knives fashioned out of spoon handles. How disgusting the gray- and blue-striped prison suits and clownish berets. How nauseating the battered bowls out of which we slurped up the thin liquid they called soup and coffee, taking turns with two or three of our comrades. Yellow triangles and number patches. Yellow stars of David bearing the word *Jude, Jood, Juif* or simply the letter *J*. Prayer shawls and phylacteries that had outlived their owners. Drawings and notes that had defied destruction because they had been stuffed into cracks, hidden between beams, or buried under rubble.

Bonnie G., a heavy-set woman with gray hair, strode towards me with firm steps and greeted me kindly. She led me to another room, all the while giving instructions to her young assistant.

The archives were crammed with so many books, files, tapes, cabinets, tables, scanners and audio-visual aids that there was barely enough room for her desk and the chair she invited me to sit on. But a weight had been lifted from my shoulders: no pictures, no display cases!

We hardly had time to exchange a few pleasantries before she was interrupted by an urgent message. She got up and squeezed past her desk. "Would you excuse me? I'm afraid I'm going to have to leave you for a moment. Mrs. Eliach is calling from Washington."

Oddly enough, the relaxed atmosphere I ordinarily associated with archives was absent here. Instead, they appeared to be working frantically to catch fleeting time by the tail. Hundreds of tapes bore witness to a relentless desire to collect the stories and testimonies of pious survivors before death snatched them from posterity.

Before coming to the US I'd read several of these stories, edited by the woman now on the phone from Washington. She'd entitled it *Hasidic Tales of the Holocaust*. Every chapter, every page had confronted me with facts I'd encountered in countless reports and archives as well as in my own memory. However, the images in this book were steeped with the enigmatic and mystical warmth of Singer and Chagall, which my heart understands but my head does not. Nothing was attributed to chance. Every life that was saved was God's mercy. Faith radiated from every sentence.

My own images are chilling, bleak and frequently gruesome – tiny islands of hope and camaraderie in an ocean of rage. The words surrounding me in this archive were, despite the tragedy, words of faith and hope, confirming the traditional Passover stories: Deliverance from Slavery, the Exodus of the Chosen People.

The anger and fear that had overwhelmed me when I'd first entered the room and been confronted with the mementoes of my youth had gradually subsided. What right did I have to judge these displays in terms of masochism and flagellation? Now that my nerves had calmed down a bit, I realized that for Hasidic Jews these objects and photographs had another, almost ritualistic meaning. Like the pictures in the *Haggadah*, the story of the flight from Egypt, they were saying, "Despite the humiliations heaped on you by man, Yahweh will not let you down!" This thought was a source of comfort to many people both during and after the war, though not to me or others like me. I'd been surprised and moved in Eliach's book to see chance disguised as mercy, and rescue from the fire-storm elevated to a reward for unshakable belief. However, the arrogant assumption that only a few could be chosen had gradually begun to grate on my nerves. But here, in this cramped space, where thousands of voices have whispered their stories onto tape, I realized more clearly than ever that this Talmudic belief had kept many from the black despair that had cost others their lives.

During the tea break, where peace and quiet reigned, Bonnie asked me to explain what I hoped to find in her archives. She patiently helped me search the card catalog for the names and addresses of people who may have crossed my path during the war, or even traveled part of the road with me. Our efforts bore little fruit: my list of survivors was no longer than when I started.

She walked me to the exit. When I mentioned that my next appointment was with Harry G. in New Jersey, she stopped dead in her tracks. She repeated his name and asked in an awestruck voice: "Do you know who his wife is?" When I shook my head, she exclaimed dramatically, "She's the daughter of one of the most pious and learned Hasidic rabbis in New York. A princess from a famous dynasty!"

Our farewell was friendly but formal: "We'll be in touch."

I walked back to the subway station. From its great height, I looked down at the building I'd just come from. At the black and white movie below. At the shtetl in the New World, where the Talmud was the guide to everyday life.

*

In the graffiti-covered train, filled with nodding junkies and snoring drunks, I ride back to the modern age, in which I feel as homeless as in the unwalled ghetto I'd just left behind.

Click clack . . . click clack . . . click click click clack . . . click clack . . . click click clack: the melody of the rails and switches is mildly hypnotic. Though the trip to Edison, New Jersey takes only an hour, it seems much longer because of the stark industrial landscape outside my Amtrak train. Harry and I had arranged over the phone to meet at the Metropark station. Only now does it occur to me that we hadn't agreed on a sign of recognition.

I try to imagine him in a caftan and hat. And his wife, the princess from the Hasidic dynasty, in a black dress with white stockings and a wig or kerchief.

Metropark turns out to be a sunny modern commuter station with a sprawling parking lot, where gleaming American cars are patiently awaiting the return of their affluent owners from the New York business world.

The midday sun has warmed the concrete bench in the waiting area to boiling point. There's not a person in sight. The air shimmers above the asphalt and the scraggly bushes in the traffic island. As I head for the shade I hear the swish of car tires behind me. Then another silence. I turn around and see that the driver is observing me from behind the tinted windows of a luxury car. He opens the door and gets out. A stocky, almost athletic man in an impeccable navy-blue suit, pale-blue shirt, and tie remains standing beside the car. We look at each other. My eyes explore his face: his broad cheekbones, his stubby, non-Jewish nose, his dark, alert eyes, his thick black hair, combed back from his forehead and just starting to go gray – and his numerous wrinkles, which could mean either seriousness, humor, or distrust. Nothing reminds me of the boy I once knew, and yet I instinctively feel it must be him. Hesitantly, almost involuntarily, I ask: "Harry?"

A smile broadens his already broad face, then gets drowned by a wave of emotion. Wordlessly, we walk towards each other and embrace; long-lost brothers.

In the car he apologizes for not answering my letters and lengthy questionnaires. His husky English hints at a childhood in Czechoslovakia, with a heavy overlay of Hebrew.

We drive through Edison's beautiful, broad streets. Not a ghetto like Brooklyn, though mezuzahs are clearly visible on most of the doorposts. He deliberately points them out to me, adding that here, in America, you don't have to hide your identity. He feels free here, free to do as he pleases.

His work – he's an executive with a large cosmetics firm – takes him to wherever makeup is sold. He's not even afraid of going to Germany these days. Grinning, he tells me how some German managers had once paled when they discovered that he could follow every word of their shady dealings.

Harry stops the car in front of a large house with a tidy lawn and privet hedge. His wife Lina is due home soon from her work. She's a nurse, in charge of elderly Jewish patients in a nearby geriatric clinic.

He takes me on a tour of the house, not to show off the split-level architecture or the comfortably furnished rooms, but to give us both a little respite. When we reach the guest room, I unpack my tape recorder and writing materials. He tenses immediately. "Let's wait till after dinner," he pleads in a soft voice.

We settle ourselves in the dining room with two tall glasses of juice. He shakes his head in wry surprise and mutters, partly to himself and partly to me, "It's been more than forty years. I hardly ever talk about it anymore. I've forgotten a lot. Well, I *wanted* to forget. I've started a new life. We need to look forward, not backward."

I hear the click of the front door and the thump of grocery bags on the kitchen table. A few seconds later Lina is standing before me: short, plump, and friendly. Her face, with its lively eyes and high Slavic cheekbones, is wreathed with thick auburn hair. All telltale signs of gray have been rinsed away. Is this the Hasidic princess? Yes, but not the Old World type I'd feared.

There's no need for Harry to introduce me – Lina knows who I am. She asks me how I'm doing, how my trip was, how my search is going. Then she heads for the kitchen to cook dinner while Harry sets the table, decorating it festively "as if it's Shabbat."

During the meal our conversation centers around unimportant things. Finally, when the dishwasher is humming in the kitchen, the second TV set is murmuring next door, and Lina is out of earshot, Harry and I can no longer avoid the matter at hand. He sits down in a dark corner of the room, huddled in an armchair. My tape recorder tries to pick up his muffled words, but his voice is so low that I have to move closer. He needs no prompting. He begins by talking hesitantly about his parents, about his childhood in Czechoslovakia before the German invasion. He clutches on to his youth in a town called Budweis.

Judaism hadn't played a role in the life of his father, a

civil engineer who owned a restaurant and brewery. Despite the Depression, they were fairly well off. His father was an active Social Democrat with friends in all levels of society, and he brought the world home with him. His family had been in Budweis for many generations, and nobody had ever made an issue of their Jewishness. His mother, born in Ostrava and raised in a traditional Jewish family, had likewise never suffered from anti-Semitism.

Until the war Harry's life had been quite normal. His school years were like those of thousands of other Czechoslovakian children. He and his friends played in the streets and fields and roamed through the woods.

The German invasion of Poland in September 1939 left a deep gash in their lives. Moravia, which the Nazis had ruled as a "Protectorate" since March 15, 1939, was the next to fall prey to the Waffen SS.

Within months, Harry's father was arrested because of his political activities. One day his mother received a telegram from a place called Auschwitz, then in its first month of existence as a concentration camp. Signed by SS *Hauptsturmführer* Rudolf Höss, it informed her of her husband's death.

The severed family moved in with his mother's parents in Ostrava. Crammed into an apartment with four other families, they waited for the sword of Damocles to fall. When the doors of the public schools were hermetically sealed to Harry and the many other Jewish children, lessons were improvised by Jewish teachers. For the majority of the pupils, Jewish education was a novel experience. "Hitler turned us into Jews," Harry says with an ironic grin. He adds softly: "My grandmothers were spared the trip to Theresienstadt. They died just in time. My grandfathers were less fortunate: they starved to death on the way."

He continues slowly, somberly, in a near whisper: "I've forgotten so much. All I remember clearly is the gnawing hunger, and the feeling of being treated to an almost unheard of luxury if you managed to get a little mustard on your bread. I can recall very little of our arrival in Auschwitz-Birkenau in the winter of 1943. I think it was in December. I still know my number by heart, but then I see it every day on my left arm: 169062."

I can identify with his hesitation, with his attempt to keep the lava of the past from erupting. The gaps in his memory are so familiar. They're there to protect him, to protect me, perhaps to protect us all. Silently, we sit across from each other in the dusk-filled room.

He unexpectedly continues, in the flat voice of a person under hypnosis. "I arrived in the shower room at about the same time as my mother. We were ordered to take off our clothes. I wanted to run away, and I fought with the kapos. I scratched and bit, but they held me tight. Some people were trying to hide over by the wall. You see, we knew about the gas. But they turned out to be real showers. They shaved our pubic hair and tattooed numbers on our arms. Outside, Polish prisoners in thin uniforms were shivering as they waited in the icy cold."

Once again Harry falls into mute silence. The murmur of the television and the rattle of the dishwasher merely serve to emphasize the quiet. He stares into space as if his images are being projected there.

He resumes in a barely intelligible whisper, paying little attention to chronology – snatches of horror that conjure up my own images. During a selection, he was sent to the left while his mother was sent to the right. When nobody was looking, the clerk motioned him over to where his mother was standing, to the side of those allowed to live. He and his mother were together for several months in Family Camp B II B.

The events of July 1944 – the selections, the labor transports, the liquidation of the Family Camp, our transfer to Block 13 of Men's Camp B II D – have been covered in a veil of forgetfulness. Only the things he can bear to remember pass through that fragile filter. We, his comrades, his brothers in misfortune, haven't been erased from his memory.

His words start to come more quickly: "My uncle arrived in a transport from Theresienstadt in September '44. I saw him in Camp B II E by the electric wires, barefoot and hungry. I threw him a couple of shoes and got caught by an SS guard. They made me stand for hours with my arms in the air, and then I was flogged. The *Lagerführer* sentenced me to twenty-five lashes. They tied me to a sawhorse and one of the kapos started in on me. But then Bednarek, our Polish *Blockältester*, intervened and managed to get the sentence reduced to five lashes."

I feel the ground sinking beneath my feet. Tears start running down my cheeks. I can hear his screams and see him stumbling off with his pants streaked with blood. The rest of us were forced to stand at attention in the assembly area between Blocks 11 and 13 and watch the entire spectacle, with our berets clutched to our sides and our heads turned sharply to the left so we wouldn't miss a thing.

My face is wet. I grab his hand and squeeze it tightly, as

if to comfort him after four decades. "Oh God, it was you. How could I have forgotten?"

We look at each other without a word. All of a sudden he says, almost cheerfully, "I bet you didn't expect that from Bednarek, huh? He wasn't such a bad guy, even though he sometimes went berserk and ranted and raved like a mad dog."

The shock of recognition gradually ebbs, and I sink back into my role of listener and interviewer. I ask him how he managed to come up with a pair of shoes in Auschwitz-Birkenau – and an extra pair at that – since shoes were as important to survival as bread and water. The question doesn't seem to surprise him. "From the *Sonderkommando*, of course," he replies, as though this was the most natural thing in the world. "They also used to slip me food."

The mysterious shutters of neighboring Block 11 had been nailed shut and had seemed impenetrable to me back then. We were threatened with draconian punishment if we so much as attempted to come in contact with the enigmatic army of crematorium workers housed there. This was enough to keep me and my three Dutch friends from even trying. But it wasn't just the fear of punishment that deterred us. We were terrified of the men of this "special unit," whose job it was to fuel the crematorium ovens with the thousands of victims of the gas chambers, sometimes including their own families. After six months they were slated to go up in the same flames, and they knew it. Compared to us, they lived a life of luxury. On Sunday afternoons they even played soccer with the SS. The men of the *Sonderkommando* lived in purgatory and stoked the fires of hell. Most of them were Polish Jews who'd been in ghettos and camps since 1939. The aura of death and damnation surrounding them filled us with fear.

Harry, Yehuda, and a few other boys from our group who could speak Slavic languages did manage to make contact with the isolated members of the *Sonderkommando*. "It was as if they adopted us, as if we brought their dead children back to life, as if helping us helped them cling to their humanity. They talked to us about the world of yesterday as if it still existed."

Now that Harry and I have dared to let ourselves feel, the mist shrouding our memories begins to lift. Our images are almost identical. As they fall into focus, the horror grows. The fatty stench of the smoke. The soup cauldrons that had to be dragged to the barracks. The endless begging for more. The punishment drills the SS referred to as "sport." The hanging of escaped prisoners. The occasional gifts of surrogate honey "organized" by the Russians. The daily race to the least dangerous place on the cart that we used to transport wood, stones, tar paper, and corpses. The *Muselmänner*, the goners, who filled us with disgust rather than pity since they were a dreaded sign of what the future held in store.

Harry and I have many memories in common, but not all. This is the first I've heard of Yehuda's bloody suicide attempt and his rescue by Finck, a boy who shared his bread and soup ration with the sick and didn't survive the camps. And of Thomas, one of the boys in our group, who was instantly transformed from friend to enemy the moment he donned the white armband of the kapo.

The last of our overlapping images has been etched on our brains like a steel engraving: the uprising of the

Sonderkommando in Crematorium IV. On Saturday October 7, 1944, all hell broke loose less than 500 yards away from us. At first our foggy minds were unable to figure out the meaning of the muffled explosions, the gunshots, the rattle of machine-gun fire, the shouts, the wail of sirens. Rumors were flying thick and fast, bringing us to a feverish pitch. We were torn between hope and fear. Was liberation near, or was the SS going to liquidate the camp? Later that afternoon we sank back into our usual apathy: Crematorium IV was smoldering, but the 250 men of the *Sonderkommando* had been chopped down by SS bullets and grenades. An easier death than the one awaiting them in the gas chamber.

Our stories flit through the darkness like bats. From time to time, the room is swept by the headlamps of a passing car – the revolving searchlights of a watchtower.

Harry's images begin to tumble swiftly over each other, as if he's clearing out his memory cells. The camp being evacuated to the promising roars of Russian artillery. Dying comrades left behind. The death march through snow and ice. SS guards in thick winter uniforms depriving the exhausted stragglers of their last bit of hope by shooting them in the head. Open coal cars carrying a tangled mass of people frozen into ice statues. A delay in Ostrava, where the inhabitants who approached with bread and water were forced to flee in the hail of bullets fired by the guards. Their arrival in Linz – decimated, ill, and starving.

"We stumbled through the streets, falling and getting up again under the hoarse shouts of the SS. They didn't dare shoot the stragglers in front of the townspeople, even though they coldheartedly turned their backs on us or cursed us as if we were lepers."

He seems to awake from a nightmare and continues haltingly, almost inaudibly: "I don't remember anything about the last part of the march to Mauthausen. I nearly froze to death while we were waiting outside the disinfection barracks, but I was saved by Fischer, Birkenau's notorious *Lagerkapo*. He seemed to turn into a different person after Auschwitz: from sadist to Samaritan. He helped us, the boys from the Family Camp, as much as possible. When he died, we felt like we'd lost one of our own relatives.

"One time Misha, Yehuda, Honza, Michael, and I were put to work peeling potatoes in the kitchen. We helped each other, stole for each other. A kapo caught me smuggling out some peels, and a guard kicked me down the stairs.

"I don't remember how I wound up in Wells, my last camp. The other boys were there too. Later on I was told that there were incidents of cannibalism there, but I didn't see any. Towards the end we got some packages from the Red Cross, but the guards stole most of the stuff. Grown-up men fought for the leftovers, bashing each other's heads in. We got nothing."

His monotone account, directed more at himself than at me, suddenly catches fire: past and present merge. "The shelling and the booming of the cannons jerk us out of our lethargy. Someone crawls outside and comes back stammering with excitement: 'The Germans are gone!' I fall into a deep, dreamless sleep. The next morning we go outside and walk through the gate. No guards on the watchtowers, no guards along the barbed wire. We keep on walking, stumbling. A huge tank rolls towards us. A black soldier sitting in the turret tosses us chocolate bars and candy. Two more tanks come, and then some other military vehicles. Soldiers lift us up. In the distance you can still hear the dull thud of artillery.

"In a nearby village the GIs set us down in front of an SS food depot. Emaciated prisoners and thin villagers are crawling over sacks of sugar, flour, and beans like ants, cramming food into their mouths, or stuffing it into pockets and bags. We can hardly eat. The food makes us sick. In the middle of all that plenty, we start throwing up.

"We're taken to an air force field hospital, but are too dazed to notice. Only when we wake up in the typhoid ward of the quarantine barracks does it dawn on us: we're free!"

His words, almost a joyous shout, bring Lina to her feet. She stands in the doorway, silhouetted by the light of the kitchen, and expresses her surprise and dismay that we're sitting in the dark. One flick of the switch and our ghosts vanish into thin air.

For a few moments the burden of memory is eased. Lina brings us a glass of juice, and Harry gives me a quizzical glance: should we go on? The emotions of the last few hours have taken their toll, but I know the thread shouldn't be broken. I nod.

Without looking at me, he picks up where he left off. "Except for Honza, who became violent and started acting crazy, we all recovered fairly quickly. After a few weeks we were roaming over the base, doing odd jobs, talking in broken English with the soldiers, and stealing combat rations, even though we were given enough to eat. 'Organizing' had become second nature to us.

"One time we spotted an SS guard outside the village, disguised in tattered civilian clothes. We didn't have time to turn him in, or maybe we didn't think of it. Anyway, the five of us started to beat him up. I guess we wanted to kill him. But we didn't. He fought back and managed to get away. We were too weak, or too cowardly, still unaccustomed to venting our rage.

"I was the first to be released from the hospital. I wanted to go back to Ostrava to find my family. I arrived in Vienna with a document signed by the American commandant, saying that I'd been liberated from Mauthausen. A nurse was waiting for me. We traveled by train to Bratislava, and then to Ostrava. It took days. Everybody we met along the way was friendly and sympathetic, but maybe that was because of my camp clothes and my stubbly head of hair. We reached the station in the middle of the night, and the nurse said good-bye. She had to catch a train back to Vienna.

"Outside the station a little café was still open. A couple of men were standing around talking. One of them motioned me over. I was still quite wary, but I went. They gave me a cup of coffee and asked me all kinds of questions. When the tram to my old neighborhood finally arrived, the oldest man offered to go with me part of the way. He got out at the next to last stop, shook my hand, and whispered, '*Mazel tov.*'"

Harry's voice is getting hoarse, and I wonder if I've asked too much of him. However, he waves off my attempt to interrupt and continues tensely: "I was standing on the cobblestones by the last stop. I looked around me in the morning mist and recognized every house, every stone. It was early, so not many people were up and about, and I hesitated to go to the house we'd been evicted from three years earlier.

"As soon as it began to get light, I set off. In front of me I saw what looked like an old woman, all bent over. From the back she vaguely resembled my mother, but then I'd been seeing my mother everywhere. She was going the same way, so I followed her. I started walking faster and faster, and the moment I was sure I shouted, 'Mother!' And it *was* my mother."

He coughs to hide a sob, and my eyes fill with tears. I feel a mixture of jealousy, grief at my own loss, empathy, and gratitude that his mother had been spared. Still hoarse, he says, very matter-of-factly but with a touch of irony in his voice: "And so we found each other. A happy ending after all."

Like swimmers after a race, we cling to the side and gaze back at the watery depths as we try to catch our breath. Harry shakes off his emotions. He starts skipping coldly and hurriedly through his life after the war. Not because it's late or because he has a heavy work load tomorrow, but because he thinks these years were so normal they're hardly worth mentioning. He slows down when I assure him that what was "ordinary" to him is exactly what interests me: the "ordinary" is so extraordinary.

His mother and her sister, who'd been liberated before he was and had come back to Ostrava, surrounded him with love. But the land of Kafka was full of ghosts, and new ones were gathering on the horizon. The two women were filled with dread. His aunt moved to the US.

His mother wanted to immigrate as well, but she preferred Palestine. For a while Harry tried to catch up on the lost years of school. He also had his Bar Mitzvah, two years later than Jewish custom normally calls for.

In the spring of 1946, a year after liberation, his mother was sent to Strasbourg as a counselor for a group of orphans, and Harry went with her. In November 1947 the two of them were given an opportunity to enter Palestine, despite the British blockade. They jumped at the chance.

Harry volunteered to join the Haganah, but was rejected because he wasn't old enough. "The camp years didn't count double," he grins. "The War of Independence in 1948 changed all that. In the mornings I worked for the air force as an orderly, and in the afternoons I was given basic training. After my eighteenth birthday this became a duty rather than a favor. Unfortunately, they kept me on the ground: I became an airplane mechanic. Still, when my time was up I signed on again.

"I married the redhead I'd fallen in love with in the youth hostel in France. Her father, the rabbi, had gone to the US directly from a Displaced Persons camp, so he couldn't come to the wedding. My mother was there, but soon after that she moved to the US and remarried. We'd applied for immigration right after the war, and the papers finally came through. Lina and I stayed in Israel. We'd grown to love it because it was *our* country.

"In 1952 we decided to visit my mother. Our request for visitors' visas was turned down, on the grounds that I had an immigration visa but Lina didn't. We had to wait four years, but they finally let us in. The absurdities of bureaucracy!

"With our visitors' visas in our pockets, we set off for

America, though we hardly had a dime. We were planning
to stay only three months, but I decided to look for a job
so we could save up a little money. Besides, I didn't want
to sponge off my mother the whole time. However, things
don't always turn out the way you planned. My visa
allowed me to work, and I quickly found a job as a tech-
nician at the company I'm still working for. Just before the
three months were up, I gave notice. We'd already
arranged everything for our trip back. But they offered to
double my salary if I'd stay for six months.

"We got used to the higher standard of living, the peace
and quiet, the American way of life. I was promoted every
year, and my salary rose accordingly. There was no
rationing here, no shortages, no danger of war. We felt
safe, but also guilty. We still do. To us Israel will always be
the Promised Land. We don't have any real friends here
like we had there. But our sons and our grandchildren
have grown up here."

As if to justify his choice, he pulls a couple of pictures
out of his wallet and shows them to me: young American
intellectuals and their slender, well-groomed wives, frolicking with their well-fed toddlers on neatly tended lawns.

The next morning Harry and I sat quietly at the breakfast
table. My head was pounding after a dream-laden night. I
lacked the energy to put the flywheel of words back in
motion. Lina, still in her bathrobe, looked tired and
troubled. She watched us anxiously, afraid that our ghosts
would exact too high a toll. Harry ate hurriedly, staring
blankly into space. He furrowed his brow, a sure sign that
he was thinking about something. Probably not his work.

We waved good-bye to Lina from the car. She leaned

against the silver mezuzah on the doorjamb and waved her handkerchief as if to dry it after our farewell. For the first few miles we were swathed in the silence of an unfinished conversation. The motor purred reassuringly, but I felt that Harry was searching for words. He pulled over to the side of the road and switched off the engine. Without looking at me he said, "Actually, I never talk about those years. What happened last night wasn't real. It can't be. I'm an optimist. I take a positive view of mankind. We're making progress. People are becoming more intelligent, better educated. Crises and depressions may come and go, but the level of prosperity is constantly on the rise. The standard of living keeps going up. Technology points the way. It's an exciting time to be alive."

For a moment I was too stunned to speak. The last thing I expected was this gossamer-thin mantle of self-protection. I knew I should leave it intact, that I should keep my sarcasm to myself. But I couldn't help asking him why he thought we survived, and in his words I recognized the chinks in my own coat of mail.

"We just happened to be in the right place at the right time. Maybe the support we gave each other upped our chances a bit. Perhaps it's made us tougher than other people, better able to put things into perspective. I really admired Finck, who shared his bread with the sick. I thought he was a saint. But wasn't he also motivated by self-interest? I don't have any heroes anymore. If you ask me, everyone likes himself best."

Our farewell at the station was short and affectionate. He waved briefly, then drove off to work, to watch over the production of the cosmetics the world demands for its adornment.

DISPLACED PERSONS

All three of them had smiled into the camera. The one on the left with a toothy grin, his eyes shut. The one on the right with his eyes half-closed, his lips turned up just enough to expose his two front teeth. The one in the middle looking mockingly at the lens, his mouth set in a grim smile. Their ears stuck out too much, like dish antennas attuned to danger. Unbuttoned shirt collars accentuated their thin necks and prominent Adam's apples. Their smiles made me wince; I could feel how forced they were. I was reminded of Kurt Tucholsky's "*Lerne lachen ohne zu weinen*: [Learn to laugh without crying]."

The photograph had been taken thirty-five years ago. I hadn't been able to identify the boys or find out where they'd come from. I was sure of only two facts: that they'd survived the ghettos and camps and that they'd lost their parents. Between 1947 and 1949 they and many others like them had sailed to Halifax on the *Aquitania*, a latter-day Noah's Ark shuttling back and forth between Europe and the New World. The Canadian government had promised a thousand children a future with a glimmer of hope.

Dozens of Canadian Jews, for whom the war had been

little more than an unsettling news bulletin from faraway, lined up on the quay to greet the arrivals. The enthusiasm of some dwindled perceptibly when they noticed there were no cute little girls for them to adopt. Only adolescents walked down the gangplank, and they seemed more like adults, since their youth had been swallowed up by the inferno.

Some of the boys I'd known in the camps had also disembarked in Halifax. During the cordial reception, cameras had clicked like an orchestra of woodpeckers. And three boys, their arms around each other's shoulders, had grinned sardonically into the camera.

A little background information might help explain the dog-eared photograph in front of me.

June 22, 1940: the capitulation of France. German and French generals are gathered around a long table in the same wooden railway car in which German aggression had been punished twenty-two years earlier. Hitler's eyes are gleaming with triumph and revenge. He and his interpreter are sitting beside Göring, Raeder, Brauchitsch, Ribbentrop, Hess, Keitel, and Schmidt – the arbiters of evil awaiting the acquiescence of the vanquished. The French general Charles Huntziger hesitates but under Keitel's threats finally signs the terms of the armistice, turning France into both a victim and a puppet of the Third Reich.

Less than four months later the head of the collaborating Vichy regime, Pierre Laval, issued a decree in which Jews were banned from public office, barred from professions, and excluded from cultural life. The Germans took this to mean that "Vichy" had embraced the Nuremberg Laws with open arms.

On October 4, 1940, one day after he'd devalued the status of every Jew in France, Laval declared open season on foreign Jews. René Bousquet, the head of the French police and a Nazi sympathizer, ordered approximately 4,000 Jews without French passports to be interned in occupied France, and 20,000 to 30,000 in the "free" zone in the south.

Berlin greeted the news with glee. Hitler, Himmler, and their man in Paris, SS General Karl Oberg, requested even more far-reaching measures. The Vichy government was not only able, but more than willing to cooperate with deportations.

Laval and his henchmen had not failed to notice that "resettlement in the East" was a euphemism for death. Though he could hardly wash his hands in innocence, Laval put on a show of patriotism for his loyal countrymen, promising that native French Jews would not be deported or arrested by French policemen. A sham from beginning to end, since he left the roundups to the German military police. Then, without batting an eyelash, Laval had his gendarmes arrest the thousands of stateless Jews who were rotting away in notorious internment camps such as Gurs. They were then handed over to the Germans. As a reward, he was granted considerably more power in the Vichy government.

In the beginning of June 1942 Bousquet and Heydrich agreed that the German police would have free rein in occupied France, but that in Vichy France only the gendarmes would be allowed to hunt down foreign Jews.

Though Laval was afraid there would be growing resistance to his policy and that even more people would go into hiding, he was prepared to cooperate fully with the

"Final Solution to the Jewish Question." According to French law, children of stateless parents were French citizens, but Laval couldn't be bothered with such trivialities. Only at the beginning of the mass deportations were mothers with children left alone.

Oberg, anxious to fill the cattle cars to the East, kept demanding more and more human sacrifices. Vichy, fearing that there would be a public hue and cry and that the Maquis would retaliate if French children and their mothers were dragged out of hiding, ordered families to be split up. Thousands of heartrending scenes were played over and over again in the last weeks of July 1942. All across the "free" zone, mothers were torn from their children and children from their mothers. Families were scattered like grains of sand after a storm.

Adolf Eichmann came to inspect the progress. Afterward, SS *Obersturmführer* Theodor Dannecker of the Paris *Judenreferat*, the Department of Jewish Affairs, was able to report to Berlin that President Laval had no objection to deporting children.

The Vichy government didn't have the faintest idea of what to do with the thousands of orphans it had on its hands. High-ranking collaborators in the police department complained bitterly to Heinz Röthke, Dannecker's successor. On July 20, 1942, Eichmann gave the signal: old people and children were to be put on transport. The diabolical circle had been closed. Three weeks after their parents had been sent to their final destination, the children were crammed into boxcars, eighty or a hundred to a car, and shipped to Auschwitz.

They vanished almost without a trace.

*

One of the few who managed to escape the bloodhounds was a ten-year-old boy named Saul Friedländer, whose parents hid him in a Catholic seminary just before they were arrested. In his moving book *When Memory Comes*, he describes the events of that terrible summer with barely disguised anguish.

In the meantime, vague reports of the deportations and the orphans were trickling in to the Allies through various channels. Like their governments, the Jewish organizations on the other side of the ocean were unable to grasp the magnitude and gravity of the situation. Relief actions were haltingly set in motion. Protests by the French clergy and personal pleas to Laval had no effect.

Rafael Trujillo, the dictator of the Dominican Republic, offered to accept 3,500 children. The Canadian government, pressured by the Canadian Jewish Congress, immediately resolved to accept 1,000 orphans. However, the constitution required an Order in Council to be ratified by each province. A CJC representative made a whirlwind tour of the provincial capitals. Sympathy smoothed the way, and bureaucratic obstacles melted like snow before the sun. On October 2, 1942, Ottawa officially declared its readiness to accept the children. Unfortunately, they'd been reduced to ashes a month before that.

For decades, Jewish relief agencies in the US and Canada had been instrumental in getting victims of discrimination, persecution, and pogroms out of Europe. However, what was happening between 1939 and 1945 was so awful and on such a large scale that most of the people in charge of these agencies were simply unable to comprehend it.

After Germany capitulated, the gates to the camps and ghettos were opened, and the survivors were either repatriated or put into reception centers for displaced persons, where they awaited an uncertain future. National and international agencies swung into action to salvage what they could. The CJC appealed to the Canadian government to offer camp orphans a new future in Canada. Just as in 1942, compassion moved mountains. The Order in Council was still standing, and it was put into effect in April 1947: 1,000 orphans under the age of eighteen would be allowed to enter the land of milk and honey, provided the Jewish community would guarantee their financial security and make sure they were supervised by professional child-care workers.

The CJC snapped up the offer, since time was of the essence. Within a month CJC members were arriving from all over the country to attend a conference in Montreal, where they discussed what steps needed to be taken. All kinds of practical and logistical questions arose. Who would take care of the children? What were the adoption criteria? Who would pay for what? How would the children get to Canada? How would they be selected? What was their background? Were they really who they said they were?

To save time a CJC representative was sent to Europe to reserve space on the Cunard Line and obtain the required entry visas from the Canadian Immigration Service in London.

An illusion was shattered in Paris: there was only a meager supply of victims – much fewer than the industrious CJC representative had expected. Not because so many orphans had already found a home in the Old or New World, but because only about 4,000 children under the age of eighteen had actually survived the slaughter in Europe.

The CJC representative was offered a mere 150 orphans. South Africa, Australia, and Israel (or Palestine, as it was then called) had already sent out their own agents to offer the orphans a future. Many of the children opted for Israel, since it appeared to be warm, friendly, and safe, despite the British blockade and Arab saber rattling. It was also backed by a well-run organization. Set up by Henrietta Szold in 1934, it had rescued many children from the clutches of the Nazis and provided them with loving care.

The countries in the East Bloc were reluctant to send their Jewish orphans, who'd been in orphanages and sanatoriums since their release from the camps, to the "capitalistic" West. Was there no end to the Via Dolorosa? The children had become the POWs of the Cold War. However, they were immune to indoctrination, euphemistically referred to as "Marxist re-education." Years of persecution and captivity had taught them to see through the hypocrisy of political slogans.

Caregivers in both Eastern and Western Europe were loath to expose their beloved charges to the rigors of immigration. Confronted with all these problems, the CJC decided to accept only those orphans who specifically stated that they wanted to go to Canada. That cut down on the number of small children and toddlers, to whom Canada was a word like any other, but it did hold out promise to the older ones.

Refugee-assistance programs gradually began to place

their trust in the CJC representatives. Visa requests started flowing in, even from the East Bloc. Still, the wheels of bureaucracy turned slowly. Hurdles in the form of screenings, security checks, and medical exams led to delays or proved to be unsurmountable for many. In the beginning of 1948 slightly more than 1,000 children were ready to go. The CJC had exceeded its quota, but the government in Ottawa kindly relaxed its standard. In the end exactly 1,116 orphans were allowed to pass through the gates.

Professional child-care workers and interested laypeople worked hard to find families who would make these children feel at home. They looked at age, country of origin, and religious beliefs: observant with observant, non-observant with non-observant, agnostics with agnostics.

This attempt to regulate supply and demand created a lot of tension between the children and the foster parents, not to mention between the professionals and the philanthropists. Much love and care was lavished on the orphans, but many of them were misunderstood. After six years of war, repression, and deportation, after six years of beatings and gassings, after a daily reality of slave labor, starvation, theft, plunder, and murder, they were no longer young and innocent. Parental authority was something out of a distant past. Love and tenderness were threatening and unfamiliar.

Some families managed to break through the wall of incomprehension. In others it remained as hard as granite. A number of kids drifted from one city to another, from one foster home to another, from one job to another. Only a few managed to adjust completely to the language and customs of their host country; for many it required too much strength. Only rarely did one of them achieve social success, academic excellence, or great wealth. Years later these exceptions were proudly trotted out by the Canadian press as proof that Canada is a land of golden pportunity. The drifters, the emotional cripples, and the suicides were forgotten. Those who had managed to blend in, by far the largest group, were ignored. After all, assimilation is "normal" and lacks the appeal of glittering stardom.

To understand the photograph of the three boys, we need even more information. After all, what's "normal" after the inferno?

Outside the baggage-claim area, a group of people were holding up cardboard signs. They shifted their weight from one foot to another or walked slowly back and forth. A demonstration against one of my fellow passengers? Against noise pollution? The controversial candidacy of the governor of Massachusetts?

I took my bags from the carousel and moved towards the silent crowd. Only then was my imagination brought down to earth. Not demonstrators, but people collecting passengers. The signs were meant to attract the attention of friends or lovers, relatives or business acquaintances, familiar or unfamiliar faces.

As the number of hugs and handshakes grew, the signboard forest began to thin out. When only a few were left on the perimeter, doubt began to creep in. Would Misha K. and I recognize each other? Was he too embarrassed to use the trappings of a demonstration? Had he actually come?

Strolling among the waiting and the awaited, I spotted a serious-looking man over by the counter. A scholarly type with a pale, narrow face, glasses, a neatly clipped moustache, and gray hair. At chest height he was holding a placard with my name printed in block letters.

We greeted each other awkwardly, almost shyly, without a spark of mutual recognition. On the way into Boston I inundated him with stories of my trip. He drove downtown and parked the car. In a burst of enthusiasm he gave me a tour of "his" city, pointing out exciting new buildings, a lovely park with a pond and the cathedrallike Christian Science complex. When he saw that I was genuinely interested, despite my tiring plane trip, he became animated and told me about his work as an architect and designer of modern buildings. For the time being we left the theme of my journey untouched.

On the way to his house in Brookline, one of Boston's wealthier communities, he chatted about his wife Ilana's busy but satisfying job as a pediatrician, his daughters and their progress at well-known Ivy League colleges, a vacation in Czechoslovakia, future plans. Not a word about the past, not one false note about the war, not a single allusion to the Shoah.

His house, high up on a corner overlooking the intersection of two streets like a lookout tower, was simple and a bit old-fashioned, a seeming contradiction to his love of modern architecture. We climbed a sloping garden path, past fruit trees and tomato plants, until we came to a glassed-in sun porch. A table had already been set for lunch. "Or would you rather eat outside?" he asked. A purely rhetorical question, I assumed, since the overgrown yard hardly lent itself to picnics.

Ilana came outside. Short, gray-haired, sturdy. No makeup, no frills. She gave me a searching but friendly look and shook my hand. During lunch she led the conversation around to my flight from New York to Boston, the beauty of the coastline, their vacations in Cape Cod, my children, their children, my house, their house, my city, their city.

When the youngest daughter, Dana, came in Misha introduced me as though I were a colleague from the Old World. She sat down across from me. A nice, round-cheeked, curly-haired coed with a shy look in her eyes.

All of this eloquent silence about the purpose of my visit was making me nervous. I could no longer restrain myself. I looked at her and said, with my mouth full, as if to cushion the blow, "Your father and I were in the same camp." Her eyes opened wide. It was so quiet you could have heard a pin drop. She whispered that she'd guessed as much.

The ban was broken. Misha explained that I'd come to question him about that period in our lives, but Dana turned to me and asked how much I remembered, what I was going to write about, and why I was only doing that now, after so many years had gone by.

Ilana's face was lined with worry. Although Misha was pale, he'd dropped his mask of self-control. I told my story, and he nodded occasionally, as if he were suddenly reminded of something.

My life "before" and "after" was quickly told. The men in our group may have been driven out of a wide variety of villages, cities, and countries, but our experience of persecution and war, deportation and camp, liberation and a homeless homecoming follows a nearly identical blueprint. Our lives after 1945 – our adjustment or mal-adjustment, our success or failure, our repressed memories or cries for help, our resignation or rage – range from one end of the spectrum to the other.

I talked about the time, not so long ago, when I began to face up to my own past, and how I'd set off in search of the others to see how they'd survived the catastrophe and had managed to go on living.

Dana hung on to every word. A blush appeared to spread over her face as her eyes filled with tears.

I strung one sentence onto another, barely paying attention to my train of thought. All at once I came to a screeching halt – lost in my own story. In these orderly surroundings, where everything seemed to run like clockwork, my words sounded mechanical or, even worse, ridiculous. I tried to switch to a neutral subject, failed miserably, and lapsed into silence.

At the end of several long bashful moments, Dana stood up and started gathering her things together. It was time for her to go back to college. She kissed her parents goodbye, then came over to me. She hugged me shyly and stammered, "I think I have a better idea of why my father never told us anything. I hope you find what you're looking for."

That afternoon it's deathly quiet in the house. Outside, an occasional car revs its engine or brakes at the intersection. Misha is sitting across from me. The dining-room lamp, switched on earlier than usual, is shining down on a stack of old, yellowed exercise books. My tape recorder is whirring away, and I'm clutching a thick questionnaire. I feel like an examiner, a role that doesn't suit me and one I'd hoped to avoid on this trip.

I start by asking Misha about his background. His

answers are detailed and accurate, but spoken in a flat monotone, as if every emotion is taboo. If I hadn't known that most of his immediate family had been annihilated, his description of his youth in Czechoslovakia would have sounded perfectly normal, conventional even. His father had been a doctor in the industrial town of Nachod. Politics hadn't interested him very much, though he had done what he could for the poor. His mother had been fairly observant, but since his father no longer was, Misha had been allowed to go to a public school. Until the Germans invaded Czechoslovakia, Judaism hadn't played a significant role in their lives. He smiles and says, echoing Harry G. in New Jersey, "Hitler turned me into a Jew on March 15, 1939, the day his troops crossed the border."

I know what he's referring to, but am surprised at his mentioning the exact date. "Early that morning," he continues, "the soldiers were standing in the marketplace, shivering in the snow outside the window of my aunt's house. She was old and didn't realize that they were Germans, so she gave them a cup of soup. When she found out what was happening, she took an overdose of sleeping pills. She was the first victim in our town."

From then on the freedom of the Jews was whittled away inch by inch. His family took in various relatives, but a year and a half after the invasion they were all forced to move to a run-down house with no running water in the Jewish quarter, the Židovská Ulice.

One year later they and hundreds of other ghetto-dwellers had found themselves waiting in the snow with their knapsacks and bulging suitcases for the train that was to take them to an unknown but frightening destination: Theresienstadt. A handful of gendarmes and one or two German guards were all that was needed to maintain order. There was no point in trying to escape. Maybe it was even safer there?

Misha's narrative starts to lose momentum. He stares into space, trying to squeeze the facts from his memory, shrugs, and confesses hesitantly that he remembers nothing of the time he was in the camps.

The exercise books on the table contain a report he wrote soon after liberation, on the advice of the doctors in the sanatorium in the Tatra Mountains where he was sent to recuperate. Whenever I ask him something about the period from December 12, 1942, to May 7, 1945, he admits with embarrassment that he can't remember, then leafs nervously through pages filled with childish handwriting. He shows me the notebooks, and though I can't read Czech I recognize many of the scenes he drew in simple but revealing sketches: barracks, guards and kapos, prisoners being counted during roll call, beatings, hangings, SS men with whips and rifles, a selection, a crematorium, barbed wire dotted with insulators, Mauthausen's main gate.

My questions about the past taper off into silence. Why should I strip away his comforting cloak of forgetfulness? He'd already liberated himself of that poisonous burden in the sanatorium. I almost envy him.

Elie Wiesel's secretary asks us to wait. A group of young Hasidim are chatting noisily outside his office. Her constant reminders to them to lower their voices only helps for a little while.

Wiesel's invitation to meet him at Boston University had reached me right before my departure. I hadn't known him at Auschwitz, but as child survivors we have a bond that makes a personal meeting possible. After I arrived in Boston, I asked Misha to share the honor of this visit with me. He too is an admirer of Wiesel's work.

Before long, the two of us are seated across from the man whose first book, *Night*, had managed to put into words the screams that filled our hearts, the hearts of everyone who shared his fate. My tongue-tied awkwardness melts under his friendly and melancholy gaze. He shows an intense interest in my search and my plans.

Almost as an imperative, he tells me to write. To describe how we live. How we live with *it*. The same question permeates his own life and work. He enthusiastically quotes the historian Emmanuel Ringelblum, who carefully jotted down his observations in a diary that he kept until his death in the Warsaw ghetto uprising. He also reminds us of Simon Dubnow's injunction to use stories and writings to hold on to the past. His words help ease the strain and anguish of my search.

We part as friends. My desire to forget has vanished.

The next afternoon I once again take up my position across from Misha, questionnaire in hand. We begin where we left off. He reads a few passages from his exercise book, describing the end of the war, when he and a few of the "boys" lay weak and exhausted in tents in Gunskirchen near Mauthausen, listening to the artillery of the American armored division, not knowing whether death or liberation would reach them first. His diary tells little about their liberation – he was unconscious most of the time and too sick to notice what was going on.

While recovering in an American air force hospital near

Hörsching, he found a couple of friends whose lives had likewise hung by a slender thread. He describes how one of the boys in his ward was reunited with his father, a doctor who'd traveled with the Allies in hopes of finding his son. We look at each other, barely able to hold back our tears. The same thought flashes through our minds: "Why him and not us?"

His return to Czechoslovakia was like that of most survivors. No parents, hardly any relatives, an occasional acquaintance, maybe a distant aunt or uncle. A foster family that surrounded you with warmth was a godsend.

The events of February 1948 filled the homes of the returnees with fear and insecurity. Stalin's terror cast its shadow over everything. The speeches of Klement Gottwald and his Communist cronies spelled disaster to the children of sheltered bourgeois families. The Reds occupying "The Castle" were at best indifferent to the fact that these children had spent their youth in concentration camps and had almost no family left.

Misha studied hard, very hard, to make up for lost time and to forget - or block out - the past. But unless you joined the Party, your future was none too bright. When the CJC and the Jewish Joint Distribution Committee offered him the chance to immigrate to Canada, he accepted eagerly. His only hesitation was that good foster parents were hard to find.

From now on Misha refers to his writings in another, larger notebook. He remarks with a smile that in 1948 the paper in Canada was of a better quality than in Europe. From time to time he has to resort to the written word to jog his memory, but his story seems to flow more easily now.

"Aboard the *Aquitania* I ran into a couple of guys I'd known in the camp. We'd lost touch. Perhaps we'd been trying to avoid the past? Anyway, in Halifax we drank Coca-Cola for the first time in our lives and gawked at the big shiny cars we'd seen only in movies. We each went our separate ways. I wound up in Montreal with a family of narrow-minded Orthodox Jews from Romania. I didn't understand them and they didn't understand me. Nobody understood us. Least of all ourselves."

He stares meditatively into space, his brow furrowed. He no longer has to consult his notes. The postwar years are apparently not blanketed in a thick fog.

"In Montreal I kept on working hard so I wouldn't have to feel anything. Before long I graduated from high school and was the only one of our little group given permission to go to college. I studied architecture at McGill University. A cousin of mine, who'd immigrated to New Jersey in 1940, had advised me to apply for immigration to the US right after I arrived in Canada, but the quota was full that year. I finally got my papers in 1951 and went to live with him and his family.

"They were good to me, but I wasn't happy there. I felt like I was living in a bell jar. The world around me seemed unreal. In spite of my depression, I graduated from Columbia University. Suddenly the loss of my family hit me hard. I had a nervous breakdown, and that's when most of the camp years were erased from my memory. 'Partial amnesia,' the doctor called it. Without my notebooks, those years would be gone for good.

"I worked for an architectural firm for two years and saved for a trip to Europe. Who knows why – curiosity, homesickness, a need to look for my past, my parents?

"I was planning to stay for six months. It turned into six years. I worked for two years in London and four in Geneva. I always managed to find work in my field. I met my wife in Switzerland, where she was studying medicine. She was born in Israel, and we went there to get married in 1963. We spent our honeymoon in Prague and Nachod. I wanted to find my old world again. Later, I went back a couple of times, in spite of that awful regime." I listen in amazement to his precise and chronological account. His voice has changed; it's clearer, more sure of itself.

"Now that I had Ilana I dared to go back to the States. She did her residency in New York. We enjoyed our work, but decided New York was no place to raise a family. We've lived in Boston for twenty years. In an old house, in an old neighborhood, in an old city vaguely reminiscent of Europe, where we have decent schools for our children." Proudly, but without boasting, he sums up the achievements of his daughters.

That seems to be the end of today's session. He clears off his papers and sets the table. Ilana comes home from work and makes dinner. She's tired and doesn't talk much. I get the feeling she'd prefer us to leave the past alone. Everything seems to be perfectly normal during the meal. We chat as if I'm an old friend who just happened to drop by. Halfway through the soup, Misha gets up, collects the bowls, and brings them to the dishwasher. He repeats this performance at the end of every course, even when we're still chewing. During dessert I protest in mock dismay but, unperturbed, Misha carries on with his ritual. When he disappears into the kitchen after dinner, Ilana ruefully shakes her head and says softly, with good-natured ridicule, that we're all entitled to a few quirks.

*

The next morning we take our places at the table again. Before I can say anything, he confesses that he was bombarded during the night by thoughts and images of his buddies in the sanatorium, his "homecoming," and the empty space in his life where his family used to be. "My memory of those years might be a little hazy, but they're always there. The older I get, the more I think about it. I can remember a couple of the boys with absolute clarity. I have no idea whether it's because we traveled together to Canada or because we were friends after liberation. I only got to know Honza S., who now lives in São Paulo, in the sanatorium in Hörsching, where we were both convalescing. That's where he got the nickname Gorilla. You see, one day he went absolutely crazy and started smashing everything in sight. They had to carry him off in a straitjacket.

"I've never really been integrated into 'normal' society. I can't talk to people I meet in my everyday life about what happened. Basically, I think of those experiences as strictly personal, something nobody else has access to. This is the first time I've been able to share them with someone who's gone through the same thing. I'm nervous about the reunion that's going to be held in Israel, but I'm also looking forward to it."

Outside the window of the Greyhound bus, idyllic Grandma Moses scenes glide past me. I see blushing maple leaves, little white churches, clapboard houses in various shades of pink, green, and blue, kids biking to school in brightly colored clothes: pure happiness. The bus rolls eastward over the eight-lane highway to Buffalo through the seemingly endless hunting grounds of extinct

Indian tribes. Road signs point the way not only to places where the buffaloes once roamed, but also to antiquity: Troy, Ithaca, Syracuse. The humming engine, the melancholy landscape in the filtered light of the setting sun, and the lovebirds two rows ahead of me evoke long-forgotten melodies. Snatches of a Simon and Garfunkel song keep running through my head, and I begin humming "I've Come to Look for America."

On the horizon I see a row of slate-black books with speckled covers silhouetted against a purple evening sky. Gradually, the contours of downtown Buffalo come into focus, and the lighted windows of the skyscrapers align themselves into orderly rectangles.

The Greyhound station is filled with people. Jaded adolescents are slumped in red plastic chairs, chewing bubble gum, sipping Cokes, and looking in boredom at the TV screens attached to the armrests. Bedraggled couples are trying to lure their numerous offspring away from the vending machines. A line of impatient passengers has formed by the revolving door to the loading area – a driver is late. I go to a pay phone and dial Jindra S.'s number. His wife Benita, her voice booming through the receiver, welcomes me warmly and informs me that Jindra's on his way. He ought to be downtown in about five minutes.

A short, athletically built man in a lumberjack shirt comes towards me with outstretched arms and a broad smile. He shouts my name across the room as if we see and talk to each other every day. I recognize his American twang with its Central European cadence from our transatlantic phone calls.

We drive through deserted downtown Buffalo. The romance of the prairie is nowhere to behold, and the name strikes me as absurd. Concrete colossuses, drained of life after office hours, tower over empty streets and abandoned plazas. A lone police car slowly patrols the inner city in the falling darkness. The business district, Jindra explains, is not safe after dark. Dr. Jekyll during the day, Mr. Hyde at night.

Jindra's neighborhood resembles a chessboard. In the middle of each square is a tidy house bordered by a well-kept lawn, looking very much like its neighbor. Metal mailboxes mounted on wooden stakes are posted like pint-sized sentries beside every walkway. The streets intersect each other at right angles; curves and slopes are nonexistent here. Only the cars show any variety, though it's hard to make out the colors in the weak light of the street lamps.

As Jindra wheels his Chevy into the driveway, Benita comes out to greet me. A moment later the two of them are standing side by side in the glow of the porch light: two short people with glasses, smiling broadly, and looking oh so American.

The screen door opens to reveal a modest living and dining room. A pot of chicken soup is steaming on an electric stove in the kitchen. Jindra's mother-in-law is chopping up vegetables. She sticks out her elbow for me to shake and welcomes me with a "*shalom*."

In the guest room, where I unpack my pajamas and freshen up after the long bus ride, I hear loud voices raised in argument. As soon as I enter the living room, Jindra says with a great deal of embarrassed hemming and hawing that tomorrow is their usual Sunday afternoon football. They never miss a game. Would I rather stay home or go with them to see the Bills play Ohio? He makes it sound like a great event. Not wanting to seem unfriendly, I promise to go, covering my surprise with a show of enthusiasm, though football doesn't interest me in the least.

After dinner Jindra hunts around for some picture albums and files. Benita shouts advice from the kitchen, where she's doing the dishes. Her mother goes home, but not until they've agreed on what food to take to the game.

As I insert a new cassette in my tape recorder, my host interrupts: "Don't bother. I hardly remember anything about the years I was in the camp."

I'm assailed by irritation and doubt. Have I traveled all this way for nothing? Will I have to spend the entire evening listening to chitchat and looking at snapshots? I bow to the inevitable. But just to be on the safe side I keep the tape rolling.

Both Jindra and Benita take a seat across from me, determined to share Jindra's life with me despite the gap in his memory. He plunges in, rattling off facts about his family in prewar Czechoslovakia as though I'm a clerk in some government office: his father was a lawyer; his mother was a housewife; he was born in Teplice-Schönau in 1931; he had one brother, four years older; his last-known residence in Czechoslovakia was Prague; he had an uncle in England; his father died just before the German invasion.

All very precise, all told without a falter. The hesitation begins only when he gets to the roundups in Prague. He vaguely remembers waiting with his mother for the train to Theresienstadt, but being sent home again because the quota for that day had already been filled. Except that "home" had already been looted. Two weeks later the fatherless family found itself in the Theresienstadt ghetto.

After that the images are a blur, the dates hazy. He doesn't even remember when he and his family were deported to the Family Camp in Birkenau. I ask him what the number on his forearm was. In answer, he rolls up his left sleeve. He was known as A-1843. The tattooers had made a mistake: the 3 was first a 2. His face lights up: "My brother was A-1844. We were next to each other in line." According to his number, he and I were in the same May 1944 transport, but that too has been erased from his memory.

My specific questions don't get us any further. All he can remember of the period between the winter of 1944 and his liberation in April 1945 are two words: Dora and Nordhausen. He says the names of the two camps as though he's not sure of the pronunciation. All at once the reason for his amnesia is clear to me, and I'm shocked into silence. After all, very few people survived that hell. Dora was an underground bunker, where Hitler's secret weapon, the V-2 rocket, was manufactured by prisoners who never saw fresh air or daylight. Except for the kapos and guards, the only ones to come above ground were the dead or the dying.

Upset, I feign exhaustion. But Jindra, unaware of the havoc those two names have created in me, cheerfully continues. How he wound up in Bergen-Belsen is still a mystery to him. His mother was there. She'd kept herself alive by acting as an interpreter for the Czechoslovakians in the Women's Camp. She sent notes to Jindra, written on scraps of packing paper, and bread from her own meager ration. After the camp was liberated by British troops and he was able to walk again, he went looking for his mother.

He found her in the morgue. Dead of typhoid, after three days of freedom.

Jindra opens one of his file folders and carefully extracts a transparent envelope. Lying side by side are three crumpled scraps of brown paper, covered with tiny handwriting in pencil. He presents them to me on the palm of his hand – precious relics. For a moment he says nothing.

Then he starts talking loudly and feverishly about the orphanage in Prague he was sent to, his inadequate schooling, his uncle who came over from England to claim his father's business, his protest against his uncle's guardianship. He leaped at the chance to immigrate to Canada, though the *Aquitania* didn't depart until August 1948.

A letter was waiting for him when he landed in Halifax. His friends Robin and Martin H., both of whom had arrived a month earlier, urged him to come to Toronto. He set off with a friend called Long John, whom he'd met on the boat. Long John quickly found a good foster family, but Jindra's was cold and impersonal. He felt lonely and left out. He told his troubles to Long John, a resourceful type who'd lied about his age so he could get on the "Canada list" of orphans.

"He found a family on his street who was willing to take me in as a boarder. I felt like I'd won the lottery. They were *so* nice to me. I had all kinds of jobs in those days, and every evening when I came home from work they listened with interest to what I had to say. One Sunday afternoon, a few weeks after I'd moved in, they had a birthday party with lots of guests. The daughter introduced me to all her friends and relatives as her 'brother'!

Not a lodger or a houseguest, but a brother! I couldn't believe my ears. I laughed and cried, all at the same time. From that moment on I was their foster son, or rather their son. And I still am."

Benita, eager to finish the story, picks up where Jindra left off: "We were married in Jindra's house. His new parents were our witnesses. They think of our children as their grandchildren."

Jindra chimes in, as if it's a duet, "They gave me a sense of security. I stopped feeling like a 'survivor.' I gradually saw less and less of the 'boys.' Their problems, their thoughts, began to seem strange to me. Sometimes I even have trouble imagining *I* survived all that."

Jindra stares into space, as if he can see his past there. "The rabbi who performed the ceremony was the army chaplain for the British troops who liberated Bergen-Belsen. We begged him to say nothing about that time. It would have spoiled the party for us.

"I think of 'survivors' as the older generation, the men and women now in their seventies, who lost their families. They seem strange to me, and yet there's a bond. The term 'survivor guilt' doesn't mean anything to me. I don't feel guilty. I was barely fourteen years old."

Benita interrupts his monologue. Talking to Jindra through me, she says, half-laughing but with her voice a shade too loud, "You hardly ever discussed it with the children. Only an occasional joke. Like when they went on a school camping trip, you said, 'At least *we* didn't have to sleep in tents and make our own food.' It wasn't until much later that the children really wanted to know anything. They didn't dare ask you, but read whatever they could about the war and the persecution."

This sparks a dialogue. Jindra says in his defense, "A lot has changed since then. We talk about it more now. I've read a lot about the camps. I pore over newspaper articles and the reports of the Holocaust Center. It annoys me because they rarely mention the children who were in the camps." As if to corroborate his statement, he points to a row of books in back of me. I nod without having to turn around. My eyes had fallen on the familiar volumes the first time I'd entered the room. "I'm not as involved with the Holocaust anymore. I'm happy here in America. I went to night school and managed to get a college degree. My English is good. I like my job as director of a data-processing unit. I work with nice people. My children are doing fine. I'm an optimist, or try to be. I count my blessings."

Benita shakes her head almost imperceptibly and asks, more gently than the last time, "Don't you think you're less sensitive than you used to be? When my father died, it didn't really seem to affect you. You told my mother she ought to go back to work after the prescribed week of mourning was over." I feel embarrassed at having witnessed her reproach, but his answer shocks me so much that I forget my embarrassment. In his words I recognize my own reaction to death.

"I was never really able to mourn the death of my own parents. It's not that I've forgotten them or don't think about them. It's just that people were dying by the thousands all around us. Death was something we got used to. It never left us. Besides, who had the time or the chance to mourn?" Jindra sinks into silence. Exhausted, we leave the past for what it is.

*

Sunday morning. Loud voices accompanied by the clatter of plates and silverware in the kitchen. I'd had a sleepless night. Benita's mother joined us at the breakfast table. She and her daughter had been up since the crack of dawn, making turkey sandwiches and filling thermoses with coffee. Jindra, wearing a bold plaid shirt, stuck a Buffalo Bills cap on his head and grinned. They were as excited as little kids about to go on a school trip, while I could hardly muster a smile.

We drove off to meet the rooters' bus that would bring us to the stadium. On the way there he described their club, led every Sunday by a gung-ho Jewish ophthalmologist and his wife. These loyal Bills fans – doctors, lawyers, managers, businessmen, and their wives and girlfriends – were every bit as enthusiastic about football as he and Benita were. Jindra was childishly happy to be part of the group. All traces of gloom had been wiped off his face.

Dozens of cheerful adults were waiting with bags of provisions beside an old-fashioned school bus. They shouted greetings and cheered every time a car with new "support troops" arrived. Most of them were wearing the same red Bills cap, and the ophthalmologist had one for me too. The windows of the bus reflected my clown's face, which did little to raise my spirits. During the drive they whooped and hollered, stuffed themselves with food, and speculated on the upcoming game.

There were hundreds of buses in the parking lot. Mounted policemen in helmets directed traffic, and everybody obediently did as they were told. Eighty thousand people surged towards the gigantic stadium.

A human sea spread out over the aluminum benches,

unwittingly producing the sound of a giant waterfall. The spectators were dressed in so many different colors that the stadium resembled a Scottish tartan. The green, rectangular football field had been marked off with white stripes and numbers. Groups like ours were sitting together in rows or clusters, eating, drinking, and gesticulating wildly. Beer and pretzel vendors were surrounded by throngs of thirsty people.

A band flanked by pretty majorettes marched onto the field, and an earsplitting cheer resounded through the stadium. The rooters, including Jindra and Benita, stamped their feet with joy. In between hurrahs, they took turns explaining the rules and commenting on the pregame show. They might as well have saved their breath. I couldn't grasp the terminology, much less the game. The scantily clad cheerleaders waved their ridiculous pompoms to the beat of the blaring march music and put themselves through all sorts of gymnastic contortions. Suddenly an expectant hush fell over the crowd. They longed for the entrance of the gladiators – helmeted and muzzled simians in shoulder pads, red shirts with huge numbers on the back, white kneepants, and red socks. "Our Bills!" shouted Jindra ecstatically in my ear. The crowd roared. When the opposing team, dressed entirely in white, trotted onto the green field, they sent up another enthusiastic cheer, albeit several decibels lower.

I watched the game with a certain detachment. The players seemed intent on crushing each other, just so they could get hold of an oval-shaped ball and throw it a couple of yards further. Jindra cheered, yelled, and moaned, raised his arms for the wave, wriggled in his seat, stamped his feet, and threw his cap into the air like eighty thousand other Americans.

I suddenly realized that, deep in my heart, I envied him. And pitied him. After all, he had his New World. He'd left his Old World behind.

By the time we said good-bye on Monday morning, Saturday's conversation had disappeared, like an early-morning fog.

John F. kept his eyes on the road. There was a lot of traffic on the Niagara Falls route between Buffalo and Canada. The passenger cars were dwarfed by all the trucks. Having to concentrate on his driving didn't prevent John from chatting, pointing out sights, and preparing me for people and events in Toronto. I'd noticed his energetic staccato when I'd met him two years before in Amsterdam. I'd chalked it up to the stress of foreign travel. But he was bursting with nervous energy again today, even though his face was a stony mask. Back then, during the first hesitant steps of my search, we'd met in a bleak, impersonal hotel room and discussed our lives during and after the war. I still had the notes from our conversation, but I needed more information.

I tried to recapture the atmosphere of trust and openness, but John took refuge in the role of guide. So I dropped the past for a while. He proudly showed me Niagara Falls, roaring behind a curtain of rain. The city seemed to be built right up to the edge. Tourists in nylon raincoats shuffled along the promontory, their cameras, lens caps off, poised for the shot. John and I inched along with everyone else, until I stopped briefly to savor nature's fury. I felt an irrational need to be relieved, if only for a moment, of the burden of my task.

We headed further north, sitting silently side by side, lost in thought. The car swished past the idyllic shores of Lake Ontario, where the white storybook houses, green lawns, and scarlet trees drew my eyes from the rusting factories on the other side.

Toronto's skyline was friendlier than I'd expected. Caught in the floodlight of a setting sun, the newly built apartments along the lake, the public benches, and the sailboats reminded me of a seaside resort. John remarked that the apartments were selling for about a million dollars. "The benches have been there longer. Macek and I used to sit there and play chess. He and his brother and some of the other boys (most of whom are now living in the States) came over on the *Aquitania* with me in 1948. We couldn't afford to go out, and chess was free. Macek, who later changed his name to Martin, committed suicide about a year and a half ago. He shut himself in his garage, turned on the engine, and lay down in front of the exhaust pipe. Nobody can figure out why he used that particular method. Robin and I knew his marriage was on the rocks, but he was a cartographer, and he'd made a lot of famous aerial photographs. So why'd he kill himself with gas instead of jumping out of an airplane?"

Startled by his blunt question, I stole a look at his profile. He kept his eyes on the windshield.

His house wasn't far from Toronto's busy main street. He parked out front, in a yard that had been paved over. He owned the entire building, he proudly reported, though he and his wife occupy only one floor. The rent from the other floors allows them to travel to distant lands.

He showed me to the guest room, called a couple of friends to tell them I'd arrived, and switched on the stereo. Out of the speakers floated high, melodic children's voices, singing in Czech. Tears sprang to my eyes. I was hearing the past: the children's opera *Brundibar*, which must have been performed at least fifty times in the dusty attics of Theresienstadt. The cast had changed constantly, since one transport of children after another kept disappearing towards the East.

John listened, outwardly unmoved, as if it were one of the Brandenburg Concertos. He explained that this performance had been recorded in the Beth Theresienstadt memorial center in Israel. "I was allowed to take part in a performance once, even though I didn't have a very good voice," he said. He turned off the record player when his wife arrived with grocery bags full of food. No more "camp" themes tonight. After dinner, the two of them sat contentedly in front of the TV. Nora embroidered, John dozed off during a nature program, and I reviewed my notes on John's life.

There wasn't much else to ask. His childhood was very similar to that of Misha K. and some of the other boys: his father a highly respected pediatrician in Budweis; his mother musical and well-read; one older brother; deported to Theresienstadt in April 1942; assigned to the youth house, where Zionist counselors did their best to teach him self-reliance; transported to Birkenau in December 1943; his mother gassed along with the rest of the Family Camp during Mengele's July 9, 1944, selection, while he was sent to the Men's Camp, where we boys were put to work pulling a cart like sled dogs.

The next morning Nora and I ate breakfast together in the kitchen. John had already left for work. "The tax office doesn't care whether its employees are plagued by memories of the camps. It expects its auditors to show up for work," she commented. "My husband never stays home unless he's sick. After thirty years of faithful service, he wouldn't dare play hookey. He didn't have it easy in his adopted country. He had to start working right after he arrived in Halifax. School was out of the question. During the day he earned his living here in Toronto as a busboy, and at night he studied English and accountancy. Once he got a degree things went better. He was so happy with his Canadian passport and civil service job," she assured me with a smile. "After we were married he went on to become a chartered accountant. It didn't help his career much, but he doesn't care. We're happy with each other and with our three daughters. We love music. Sometimes he goes to concerts in New York and stays a couple of days with his cousin to catch up on all the news. He also sings in a choir at the synagogue. But, like me, he's not Orthodox."

Nora walked over to the counter and began to clean up, keeping her eyes averted from me. "My parents and I escaped from Prague after the German invasion. We arrived in Canada via Lisbon and Tangier, absolutely penniless. We had a hard time of it here as farm workers. John and I rarely talk about the war years."

I helped her with the dishes, and she steered the conversation onto more neutral territory. Afterwards the two of us went off to explore the town and the museums. She treated me like an ordinary tourist, and the tensions of the trip began to fade away.

That night when John puts on his slippers, I find it difficult to pick up where we left off and ask my remaining questions. Although John can recall the events recorded in his brain with great accuracy, he too seems loath to plumb the depths. After a hesitant start, his voice becomes detached and businesslike, as if he were talking about someone else's life. He describes the evacuation of the prisoners in open freight cars during the icy winter of 1944. The frozen corpses that were tossed overboard, the strafings by Russian and British fighter planes, the ropes used to tie the men together like a bunch of asparagus so that the "cargo" wouldn't be lost en route. The hunger, the constant thirst, the mouthfuls of snow, the "favor" of being allowed to drink a few drops of water from the train's boiler. The Czech workers fired on by the SS when they tried to toss some bread to the prisoners. The march through wintry forests after the trains could go no further.

Less than half the column reached the camp of Flossenburg alive. Political prisoners befriended them, helped them with food, put them to work in their units.

The brief thaw didn't last long. The journey continued through snow and ice, along roads strewn with the bodies of stragglers, shot to death by the guards. Guns roared in the distance. One morning, after a night in a muddy stable, there were whispers: the guards were gone. The tattered, emaciated column fell apart. Nobody knew where to go. He and a couple of other boys wandered around aimlessly, trying to discover the source of a rumbling drone. Suddenly huge American tanks burst through the clearing. They stopped, picked up the boys, and took them to a nearby group of houses. A young Yiddish-speaking officer ordered a farmer's wife to nurse the boys and promised them help. They'd been liberated – the war was over.

John stares straight ahead. He devotes little time to describing his return to Prague. "It's not important," he says. "In the town where I was born, there was no one I knew from before the war. Some nice people took me in, gave me food and clothes. The principal of the local school refused to admit me. According to him, Czechoslovakia was still governed by German law, which meant that Jewish children were banned from 'Aryan' schools.

"My father's sister came back to Prague. She'd survived because she was married to a Christian. I moved in with her and her husband, and learned to lead a normal life again. When the Communists took over in 1948, I feared the worst. So when I heard it was possible to immigrate to Canada, I immediately said yes."

He gets up to turn on the TV. I understand his need to blot out the images that are haunting him, but I have to ask one last question, however painful it may be. "What happened to your father and your brother?"

John's pale face turns ashen. He perches uneasily on the edge of the couch, stares at the floor, and mumbles, more to himself than to me, "There was this guy in Prague who promised to tell me, but then he didn't show up. I guess he just couldn't face it – the war hadn't been over very long. I only heard the story a year ago. An eyewitness told it to a distant relative of mine, and she passed it on to me. It seems that during one of the death marches in the winter of '44, my brother Karel couldn't take another step, and he collapsed. The guard kicked him and yelled at him to get up. When my father rushed over to help him, the SS man shot them both."

A resonant voice resounds through the intercom: "It's Robin." Heavy steps clump up the stairs. A tall, husky man is standing in the doorway. I shake his large hand and look up. His features seem vaguely familiar, but perhaps I'm imagining it. After all, his head was covered with stubble back then.

A stern face. Hardly a trace of a smile. He glances over at John and asks if he's told me yet.

I wonder what he means. There's an embarrassed silence. John, his voice gentler and deeper than usual, turns to me and says: "Renata, Robin's wife, doesn't want you to come to her house." I don't know which I feel more: anger, surprise, or curiosity. Surprise finally wins. I sense Robin's unwillingness to discuss the issue. He asks me who I've talked to in the US and Canada, what I've accomplished so far, and what I hope to do here. My answers elicit exclamations of skepticism that border on the cynical. However, his face relaxes as I go on. His comments become friendlier, his questions more sympathetic. Still, his quasi-interrogation annoys me. When he invites me to drive into town with him so we can talk, I'm the one who objects, and he's the one who's urging.

We settle ourselves in a quiet corner of the Toronto Hilton's sumptuous lobby. His gruffness gone, he asks me to explain the reasons for my search and apologizes for his initial distrust. He despises any attempts to sensationalize our past, but now that he realizes we agree on this point, he lowers his armor.

Seated in leather armchairs, we talk in whispers like a couple of mafiosi planning a heist. He refuses to let me turn on my tape recorder; even pen and paper bother him. I listen carefully, not letting my eyes leave his face, so I'll be able to remember everything. Gradually, as his story unfolds, I can once again picture Robin and his brother standing at attention during roll call: two giants towering above the rest. Their tall, athletic frames confused the dull-witted guards. Robin and Martin, with their flawless German and uncircumcised penises, were exceptions, quasi-Aryans. What did those SS automatons know about the variety of Jewish life? About the liberals and agnostics whose only ties to Judaism were the Jewish branches on their family trees?

Robin and Martin grew up in a family of bankers in which culture had taken the place of religion. Nevertheless, they and their parents were rounded up like all the rest and deported to the ghetto in 1942. In the dormitory of the youth house, they formed bonds that have survived even death. Robin can clearly recall the other boys. He tells me their names and describes them in detail. I can remember only a few of them, though in the course of my search I've met the handful who are still alive. The two brothers were put to work in an agricultural detail, one of the better work assignments, since you had access to food, and the living conditions weren't quite as harsh. There were even fewer casualties during the train trip and death marches.

Robin suddenly looks at me as if he wants to justify their lighter suffering: "The winter months in Mauthausen,

Melk and Gunskirchen were pure hell. All around us people were falling like stalks of wheat before a reaper. We were living in leaky tents, along with Misha, Honza, and some of the other boys. Everyone was starving. Epidemics raced through the camp: typhoid, typhus, scarlet fever, scabies, edema, tuberculosis, you name it.

"After we'd been liberated and had recuperated, we went back to Prague. Where else could we have gone? We had no one to turn to, and at least there we ran into some of our buddies who'd also made it. Honza S., my best friend, had been with us in the American hospital in Hörsching, but he went crazy one day and had to be taken to the psychiatric ward. He joined us later."

Just then our quiet corner is taken over by some rowdy hotel guests. Since our nervous systems aren't up to the noise, we agree to call each other tomorrow, and part like old friends.

The next morning, as I was trying to drown a nightmare-ridden night with a strong cup of coffee, Robin showed up, with unshaved cheeks and bags under his eyes. He got right to the point: "Renata wants to see you." His words startled me. I wondered if I'd said something to upset him. All I could manage to do was stammer "Why?"

He sat down tiredly across from me, put his chin in his hands, and said, "Renata and I talked all night long, until early this morning. I explained what you're doing and convinced her that you're not trying to commercialize the Holocaust. She hates the idea of 'Shoah business.' It scares her. She watches over my peace of mind and that of our daughter Liza like a sheep dog. I'll pick you up tomorrow. She's looking forward to seeing you." Robin left quickly so he wouldn't be any later for work than he already was. After the front door had closed, Nora confided that his position in the synthetics business was none too certain.

Renata was tall, good-looking, gray-haired, and nice. She spoke both German and English without an accent. She conversed with Robin in Czech but immediately switched to English when I joined them at the table. The walls in every room were lined with books. Kafka, Zweig, Mann, Hašek, Čapek. Russian classics. French and English novelists. Thick art books. Over dinner we discussed a Dutch Catholic poet, whose work she was reading in English, and the fresh trout that had been caught by a friend of Liza's.

They used literature and art history to fortify themselves against the miseries of war. Religion interested them, but politics was taboo. Erudition filled the room like a faint perfume, noticeable but not overpowering. Now that I could observe Robin in his own environment, I saw him through other eyes. I began to understand why he'd scorned a college education and a career. He and Renata sought comfort in other things. Some people might think of them as frills, but to Robin and Renata they were as necessary as food and water.

And yet they were curious to hear my story. They sat across from me and listened intently to my tale of a homecoming without a home and of the loneliness and adjustment problems after the horrors of our youth.

Robin unexpectedly interrupted me, his voice raw with emotion. "When Martin and I landed in Halifax, we were treated like parcel-post packages. Our group was torn apart. Luckily, my brother and I weren't split up – we were allowed to go to Toronto together. But the other orphans were spread from one end of this big country to another by insensitive social workers and CJC trustees. We didn't speak English, we didn't know a soul, we hadn't learned a trade, and we didn't have a penny to our name.

"I don't want to sound ungrateful, but the loneliness and feeling of abandonment were almost worse than the years in the camps. It nearly destroyed me, and Martin never got over his depression. As you know, he's no longer with us."

Renata went to the kitchen on the pretext of making tea, and Robin put a record on the stereo: Haydn's Emperor Quartet, the one with the notorious German national anthem. It shocked me so much that I flinched. I couldn't imagine what had possessed him to play it. Smiling sadly, he said, "Irony, humor, and, above all, beauty are the only things that make my life bearable. I hope I haven't ruined Haydn for you."

In the belly of the huge Boeing 747, I felt as miserable as Jonah in the whale. My search was coming to an end, but I didn't have a clear answer to my question of how we'd managed to go on living after the Shoah. We'd each had to fight in our own way, just to stay on our feet, but the past had weighed down on us all.

Looking out the window, I could see only the vague contours of Nova Scotia. Halifax was buried under a cloud. In the last few months a half-forgotten name from an atlas had come to life.

REUNION

His eyes, under the brim of his yellow baseball cap, roam restlessly from one face to another and scan the nametags on everyone's chest. When neither the face nor the name rings any bells, his gaze wanders further until it stops abruptly with me.

He reads my badge, looks up, and reads my name again, this time aloud. His earnest expression relaxes. He repeats my name almost ecstatically and gives me a big hug. "I'm Ernst H. from California. Oh, I'm so happy. Thanks to you I've found everyone again, and I could come to this reunion. Until I got your letter last year, I didn't know there were any other survivors." His words come tumbling out; he forgets to breathe. Touched by his joy, I throw my arms around him and stutter a few words of welcome.

We stare at each other, trying to recall what we looked like in our youth. He still speaks German with a Viennese accent. "Do you remember my cousin Walter? Who was also in our group? He couldn't come. He's not in very good health. Besides, he was a little scared at the thought of seeing everyone again." He lays down his bulky video camera, reaches into his back pocket, and pulls out a dog-eared picture of two thin boys, one in striped camp clothes, the other in shorts and a white shirt. "Now do you recognize us, Walter and me? You guys always used to call us the '*Yekkes*'* because we spoke German together." Images flash through the archives in my brain. I see him beside me, panting from exertion, our hands clutching the bars of the cart we're pushing over the muddy road behind Crematorium III.

"This picture was taken soon after capitulation by a US Army captain who had liberated Buchenwald. Walter left the camp in hopes of finding his parents, and the officer helped me get to Italy. Since none of my family was left, I'd decided to go to Palestine." His eyes turn red. He can no longer hold back the tears.

All around us there are hugs and joyful cries of recognition. Four hundred people bridging decades. We can hardly hear each other in the hubbub. Squeals of excitement and a deluge of Hebrew, Czech, German, and English. Ernst and I set off in search of faces and nametags, getting separated from our wives in the process.

I spot Yehuda B. and Dov K. standing outside the hexagonal memorial building, chatting in rapid Hebrew with two other men. When we get close enough to read their names, I realize immediately that they're one of us. Or as John F. from Toronto calls us, the "Birkenau boys." We great each other warmly, almost jovially. Like a teacher presenting a new boy to the class, I introduce Ernst. Forty-five years seem like forty-five seconds.

I leave the group and nervously scan the crowd for familiar names and faces.

The park outside the auditorium is filling with more and

* Unflattering nickname for German Jews.

more people. A year ago the Beth Theresienstadt memorial center had invited us to hold our reunion during their annual get-together for survivors of Theresienstadt. Today's meeting is extra special because it's being attended by politicians and friends of Vaclav Havel. President Havel, who was awarded an honorary degree from an Israeli university a few days ago, had brought along some of Theresienstadt's ex-prisoners in the two planes loaned him by the Czechoslovakian-born newspaper tycoon Robert Maxwell. Bursting with excitement, they're now looking for relatives and acquaintances they last saw nearly half a century ago.

Early this morning, on the way to Kibbutz Givat Chaim, where survivors and their children had founded the memorial center to house archives, photographs, and camp relics, I wondered whether I'd find Pavel B. from Prague.

I'd written to Pavel years ago, when his country was still ruled by darkness at noon, but had never received a reply. After the fall of Communism, his son had come to Holland for a conference. He told me about the isolation in which his father had lived during the last two decades, and the obstacles that had been put in his path by those in power. Pavel had originally taught history. After being ousted from his job, he went to work for Charter 77, which made him highly suspect in the eyes of the state security police. Mail from other countries often got "lost," while outgoing mail depended on the whims of the censor.

We knew that Pavel was one of the "boys" but were unable to contact him. During my search in the US and Canada for survivors of our original group of eighty-nine boys, the idea of a reunion in Israel had come up over and over again. After the fall of Communism in Eastern

Europe, the plans began to take definite shape and we agreed to attend the May 5, 1990, reunion of Theresienstadt survivors as guests of Kibbutz Givat Chaim. Tomorrow the "Birkenau boys" will have the whole day to themselves. This will give us an opportunity to draw up the balance of our lives, fifty years after we were first plunged into the catastrophe.

Rumor has it that Pavel has come to Israel in the presidential entourage. I redouble my efforts to find him, weaving my way through throngs of talking, laughing, crying men and women who are searching and finding each other. I catch sight of Dov, standing in the shadow of a tall hedge, having apparently left the circle around Yehuda and Ernst. He's talking to a black-haired man with deep-set eyes. Since they're speaking Czech, I can't follow their conversation, but it appears to be intellectual rather than emotional – two academics staring meditatively into space while they discuss their work.

Suddenly they both look in my direction, and Dov urgently motions me over. I take stock of the man beside him. My eyes search his pale-blue shirt for a nametag, but he doesn't have one. Dov introduces him, softly, pointedly, "This is Pavel, Pavel B. from Prague. He flew over with Havel."

For a moment I'm speechless. We gaze at each other, dumbfounded. Since I'd heard so much about him from his son, he's not a stranger to me. I can see from the blue tattoo on his arm, number A-1480, that he and I were in the same transport from Theresienstadt to Auschwitz.

He asks why I had my number removed and I answer, almost apologetically, that I hadn't wanted to remain an outsider forever. Mournfully shaking his head, he says, "It isn't a sign of shame, and we'll always be outsiders, no matter what we do."

Speaking schoolboy German, he chooses his words carefully. His facial muscles are not used to laughing, and when I ask him about his health, he replies hesitantly that it leaves a lot to be desired.

"Israel and all the people I've met here have really turned my world upside down. In Czechoslovakia only our thoughts were free. Any act that didn't fit the pattern set down by the dictatorship was ruthlessly punished. You were stripped of your status. We were doubly outsiders. During the freeze that followed the Prague Spring, I started researching the fate of Eastern Europe Jewry, in hopes that this subject wouldn't give offense in 'The Castle.' But after a day of monotonous and routine work, there was little time for study."

Elimelech L., who up until now had been only a name on a list, comes over and joins us. A friendly, tanned face with large glasses and thinning but still dark hair. I know little of his background. He'd returned the questionnaire I'd mailed him five years ago, but it had contained only about twenty words. The rest was completely blank. Even now he says only the bare minimum. When he mentions Nordhausen, the camp where Hitler manufactured his V-2 rockets, I understand the reason for his silence.

The babble in back of us tapers off. Hundreds of men and women, most of them elderly, start streaming into the auditorium. I find my wife, and the two of us move along with the flow, not really knowing what to expect. Everywhere I look – in front, in back, on either side of me – there's a sea of graying heads, twinkling eyes, complacent faces, gaily colored dresses, blouses, and open-necked shirts. Simple, cheerful folk: kibbutzniks and guests defying the power of the past to infect the present.

They listen intently to the speeches in Hebrew and Czech. Ernst enthusiastically films everything with his video camera, not listening. My wife and I can't understand a word. Misha K.'s wife Ilana translates bits and pieces in my ear, proud of the country of her birth. An oft-repeated theme is that of welcome and hope, as well as the desire to pass history on to future generations. I don't dare feel bored, but my thoughts begin to stray. My search will soon be over, I tell myself. Here, in this place. But what have I been searching for? And what have I found?

On the podium, a gray-haired Czech brings his speech to a close. There's a burst of applause. The speaker, a Czech attaché who's filling in for Havel, has presumably said something important. Ilana's translation confirms it: Vaclav Havel, following in the footsteps of Czechoslovakia's first president, Tomáš Masaryk, has revived the tradition of humanism in Prague Castle. Czechoslovakia has restored diplomatic relations with Israel, turned Jews into honored citizens again, and attempted to expiate its guilt by acknowledging the suffering.

Now that the official part of the program is over, the audience pours out of the auditorium in great disorder. The tension has been broken, and the sun magically wipes the seriousness from all our faces. We sit down or stroll in the shadow of the cedars, sip coffee, munch on refreshments, and pick up the thread of conversations interrupted by the speeches.

John wants to draw up an agenda for tomorrow, a series of lectures, but encounters resistance. He flits back and forth from one person to another like a butterfly, in an attempt to arrange the impossible. The form of the meeting is apparently more important to him than the content, and I feel myself getting exasperated.

In the bus, on the way back to our hotel in Netanya, I gaze at the coastline in silence. Every once in a while a dark army helicopter swoops past, following the coast. The hotel lobby is big and drafty, with large leather couches and a shiny granite floor. Behind a gleaming counter, three desk clerks are shouting into phones in a variety of languages and attending to the needs of their clamoring guests.

Our friends, adding to the chaos, ask whether the other members of "our" group have arrived and what rooms they're in. The desk clerk is harried, though not rude. Then someone mentions a name. The name of a place that sounds indecent in company, the name that only we talk about in "normal" tones: Birkenau. The clerk glances up, comes out from behind the counter, and asks John gravely, almost shyly, "Are you all . . .?" John nods and tells him, almost cheerfully, about the reunion that's brought us to Israel.

We discuss what we want to eat and which restaurant we should go to, as undecided as a bunch of teenagers on a Saturday night. Ernst, still lugging his video camera, steps out of the elevator along with his wife. He listens to our debate, comes to a swift decision, and leads us to a simple restaurant not far from the hotel. My wife and I had eaten there before, so I know the food is good and not too expensive. Ernst chatters excitedly all the way there.

Only two tables are empty. The rest are filled with talking, chewing, laughing Israelis. The twenty of us huddle around the door, peering regretfully inside.

Undaunted, Ernst addresses a waiter in fluent Hebrew, has a word with the owner, and waves us over. He helps the waiters drag in a few tables and slide them together like matching dominoes. The other diners scoot in closer, and within minutes everyone has a seat.

Ernst is bursting with excitement and joy. He'd like nothing better than to clasp each of his long-lost comrades to his chest. He and I are seated at the head of the table, and he keeps grabbing my arm and thanking me for reuniting him with his "brothers." In a booming voice he tells the waiters, the owner, and anyone else who's willing to listen why we're here. He orders wine and pours it into the glasses himself so that we can celebrate. "*L'chaim, l'chaim*: to life," we call in chorus, and for once it's not a meaningless toast.

The room is filled with a potpourri of languages. Although many of us adopted another mother tongue after 1945, Czech nostalgically predominates tonight. English is nothing more than a standby, even for Michael H., who speaks it flawlessly.

I ask Ernst where he learned such fluent Hebrew. Lapsing into the Viennese of his childhood, he tells me his life story. I knew from our conversation this morning that the death marches in the winter of '44–'45 had brought him to Buchenwald, and that after liberation he'd finally reached the shores of Palestine. I have to listen intently to keep his words from getting drowned out by the voices around me. My food gets cold. So does his. Behind the magnifying lenses of his reading glasses, his eyes are lined with grief. In shrill contrast to his euphoria.

"I got to Cyprus," Ernst says, "and found myself behind barbed wire again. The British wouldn't let us through.

Auschwitz, Buchenwald . . . they didn't care. The document signed by 'my' captain worked miracles. After a few weeks I entered Israel, coming ashore in Haifa.

"I couldn't do anything. I could hardly read, let alone write. The Germans had taken over Austria in 1938, so when was I supposed to have learned? In Israel I was apprenticed out as a welder. Once I learned the trade, I was sent all over the country with a team of fitters to lay pipes for water, gas, and oil. In 1948, when the War of Independence broke out, I joined the army. I stayed in it for five years. There wasn't much time for education, but at least I was no longer illiterate when I got out of the service.

"I crisscrossed the country again laying pipes, but this time I was foreman. I worked hard, real hard. From early in the morning to late at night. Not just because it was necessary to build up the country, but because I wanted to erase the image of my parents, my brother, my relatives . . . the chimneys. The rest of you were trying to do the same thing in schools and universities by applying yourself to your books. I didn't have that option. I used my hands, my muscles.

"I married Menorah after I left the army. She's a sabra, a daughter of The Land. We immigrated to the States in 1962. I wasn't going anywhere in Israel. After seventeen years, I'd had enough of laying pipes.

"I worked just as hard on the other side of the ocean. Maybe even harder. But now I had my own business – my cousin Walter and I were partners. We made good money. In America, you can slave away for sixteen hours a day, but in the end you have something to show for it. We started buying up houses with some friends of ours, a carpenter and a painter, and fixing them up. A couple of years ago I bought a house for $70,000. It's worth twenty times that today. Real-estate prices in Beverly Hills have sky-rocketed."

That surprises me. I hadn't expected Ernst, so full of life and yet so vulnerable, to be well off.

In the meantime, our table has become strapped for words. After a day of emotional upheaval, our faces are lined with exhaustion. We've stopped drinking wine. Even coffee fails to rev our engines. Hands start beckoning waiters. Ernst stands up and asks us, practically begs us, to let him pay for dinner. His eyes glisten with tears. "Please let me. I'm so glad I've found all of you, and it would give me so much pleasure!" He barely looks at the check the waiter sets down in front of him, but pulls out a handful of crumpled hundred-dollar bills and pays.

We're packed like sardines in the van that's transporting us to Kibbutz Givat Chaim, but no one complains. Today is our day, and inconveniences of this kind are unimportant. We observe the coastline alongside the highway in silence. The early-morning fog is lifting over the dunes, and the Mediterranean Sea is licking at the beach with lips of foam. Caesarea, once a citadel for Crusaders converting the heathen with their swords, stands out against the blue horizon. A bunch of black-haired boys are playing among the weed-choked remains of bunkers or racing after goats like a pack of dogs. Tumbledown Arab houses look woe-begone beside the uniform blocks of apartments starting to fill with Russian immigrants. Scaffolding and cement mixers are eating into the dunes.

At an intersection further inland I notice a mysterious

fort surrounded by high walls, watchtowers, and coils of barbed wire. Soldiers, their Uzis nonchalantly on their hips, are guarding a group of dark, sweating men with picks and shovels who are digging ditches around the perimeter of this unsightly structure. I assume it's an army barracks and point it out to my wife, but John promptly corrects me: it's a prison for Palestinians.

In the kibbutz, yesterday's pandemonium has made way for Arcadian quiet. Several of our friends are waiting for us in the shadow of the memorial center. Some have brought their wives, to help them keep their grip on the present as we dip into the past.

Despite the plentiful sunshine, the conference room is lit by the harsh glare of fluorescent lights. Plastic chairs are sprawled around the room. Behind the thin curtain that conceals costume changes from the audience during amateur performances, we find a table that can serve as a makeshift lectern. I'm uncomfortable with such formality, but let John take the lead. After all, he has a liking for rules and has spent months urging us to make speeches during today's gathering.

Pudgy little John, with thinning white hair, takes a seat behind the table, and the rest of us spread out in a wide semicircle. He looks searchingly around the room from under heavy-lidded but alert eyes to see if we're "all here." His high-pitched voice can be heard clearly in every corner of the room. His round, friendly face trembles nervously, but after a few words he regains his calm. He puts on a pair of black glasses, addresses us as "Dear boys," and begins his speech: "We've been granted a summer once more. During the cold winters, when I doubt if spring will ever come again, I often despair. And I wonder, as I did forty-five years ago, if I'll make it to the next day. But here we are. Fate has been good to us. We've survived – but not because of what we did, or failed to do. When I was planning this reunion, I was curious to know the reaction of the 'boys,' who have been scattered over all four corners of the earth. Would we be able to find each other nearly half a century after our rebirth? Would we still have any ties to each other? I sent out more than twenty letters, although there used to be eighty-nine of us. We're merely a fraction of a fraction that survived the forces of evil."

Just then the outline of a broad-shouldered figure appears on the other side of the frosted-glass door. Someone is unsure about coming in. All eyes turn towards the door. John stops talking. A burly man with huge hands, a thick neck, and large tinted glasses stands at the threshold and rakes the room with his eyes. He raises his hand in faint greeting. Only the Israeli residents recognize him and wave back. He and his wife come in and sit down beside me. He whispers, in the vain hope of not disturbing John, "I'm Eli B., a farmer from Moledet. I was in the same transport as you were, but I wouldn't have recognized you. Your head had been shaved back then, and you didn't have a beard." He adds with a deep chuckle: "We haven't improved any with age!" Everyone laughs. The big stranger is no longer a stranger.

For a moment the tension has been broken, but John resumes his speech in the same tone. "Despite our slow start after the war, despite the torments of depression and doubt, despite the lack of material support and the troubles in our native lands, most of us managed to build a new future for ourselves, far away from the countries of our birth."

He nods at me and goes on. "A few years ago our friend Gerhard started to renew our contacts. Like the rest of us, he suffered years of incomprehensible repression in his youth, when death and destruction threatened daily. We all have different ways of dealing, or not dealing, with our memories. Some of us have been successful, others have not, but none of us is without mental scars. Nevertheless, Gerhard has shown us that life can be – and for most of us has been – filled to the brim. We can look back at the path we've chosen with our heads held high, without shame. Our group consists of artists and intellectuals and others who worked hard with what they were given and earned an honest living. In recent months I've talked or written to almost everyone on the list. Most of us looked forward to this reunion, but there were a few who rejected the idea outright. They were afraid it might upset their peace of mind or were annoyed at what they consider to be an interference in their lives. Perhaps they think blocking everything out is better than remembering it? I'm a layman when it comes to matters of the soul, but I have the distinct impression that those who avoid this confrontation are far from happy.

"Here we are, forty-five years after the catastrophe. Most of us are married and have children, one of us even has great-grandchildren. Today we celebrate our survival!"

We sit, stricken, on our chairs. John's words weigh heavily. We're not used to thinking of ourselves in such dramatic terms. Plain words and black humor are better armor.

Dov, the youngest and smallest of the group, now a professor of modern Jewish history, is next. He's nervous. His voice is soft and hoarse. He apologizes for speaking

English and for standing up to read his research article, but explains that he's more comfortable that way, since it's what he's used to. He pulls a sheaf of typed pages from his briefcase. Then he thanks the organizers, offering his excuses for not helping with the preparations, points out that his fellow professor Pavel B. has been able to resume his work for the first time since the Prague Spring, dons his reading glasses . . . and promptly sits down.

After only a few words I recognize his speech. Years ago, the paper he's now reading in an even, unemotional voice had prompted me to delve even further into the past. It hardly sheds any new light on the historic backdrop to our stay in Auschwitz-Birkenau. After all, Mengele's selections in July 1944, the liquidation of the Family Camp, and the prelude to the drama that had entwined itself with our lives have been tattooed on our memories along with the numbers on our forearms.

Dov's friendly, gentle face is an impenetrable mask. Most of the people in the audience have retreated into their own thoughts. A few of them almost look like they're asleep. My mind begins to stray, not out of boredom, but rather out of a desire to ward off anything that might disturb my peace of mind. What are we doing here? Not refreshing our memories, that's for sure. We haven't forgotten the facts. John skirts the issues, seeking refuge in rules and agendas. Dov smothers them down in academic formalism. And I concentrate on the miracle of our postwar resurrection.

Whispers can be heard behind the glass door. Dov looks up from his paper. Sinai A., dressed in black rabbinical garb, opens the door a crack and slips into the room. He surveys the scene from under his broad-rimmed hat, smiles faintly, and nods. His wife follows in his wake, carrying his briefcase. With his modern glasses and short beard, he looks younger than he did eight years ago during our last, rather stiff, encounter. He embraces me, sits down, and signals Dov to continue. Apathy has made way for interest. All attention is now directed, almost imperceptibly, at Sinai, *our* rabbi. Faith in the middle of Doubt.

Dov quickly summarizes the rest of his speech and turns the floor over to me. Tired applause accompanies him to his chair.

John insists on introducing me and reading a letter from Ludek K., who was unable to come to the reunion because of a serious illness. A horrible thought flashes through my mind: surely John isn't going to tell them about my meeting with Ludek and the most painful moment in my entire search? Just thinking about such indiscretion makes my temples throb.

He reads the letter, recalls my visit to Toronto, and continues, without looking at me: "Ludek recognized Gerhard immediately, but Gerhard didn't recognize him. Ludek's memory is better than most of ours. He described a scene from the Men's Camp that he witnessed in August 1944. Some of you might have seen it too. After evening roll call, about ten boys decided to cool off in a water reservoir near the entrance to the camp. A couple of SS men came over and started horsing around, throwing rocks and dirt clods into the water. They noticed that Gerhard couldn't swim very well, so every time he tried to climb out of the water, they poked him with a long stick to keep him away from the edge. They were trying to drown him, and he screamed in absolute terror . . . Anyway, Gerhard had apparently forgotten this incident, or had blocked it out. He turned as white as a sheet and staggered over to the kitchen . . ."

John's story inexplicably fills me with shame. I inwardly curse him. But I get a grip on myself and, outwardly unmoved at any rate, take my place at the table. I haven't prepared a speech, and there's been no time for us to simply chat with each other. But they're radiating so much kindly sympathy that I put aside my reservations. I begin to talk about my years of silence. About my subsequent search. About my fruitless attempts to understand why we survived and how we were able to make a reasonable recovery after the war. My friends listen tensely. They recognize themselves in my questions, my doubts, my hopes. The cloud of oppression has lifted. By the time John asks Pavel B. to take my place at the table, the taboo on tears has been broken.

Pavel's voice is veiled in emotion. He confides that during the last forty-five years he knew next to nothing about us. Gottwald, Husak, and Czechoslovakia's other rulers had poisoned life for intellectuals like him. The Prague Spring seemed, all too briefly, to hold out promise. But his field, modern history, was reduced to ideological propaganda, and he loathed any kind of evangelism. He was relieved of his job at the university and forced to work with his hands instead of his head.

His fingers and hands move nervously as he speaks, as if they're kneading clay into words. His face betrays the intensity of his feelings, which he tries to hide by keeping his eyes focused on the tabletop.

He explains that he hasn't come here to speak as a historian, like Dov. He's more interested in what happened to us after the Family Camp was annihilated and the war was over. His search reminds me of my own search except that, in spite of all he'd been through in the camps, he came back religious, and I'm either unwilling or unable to accept that haven.

"I've spent years thinking about it," Pavel says. "The burden we carry is not that of Jews, but of human beings. We have a moral obligation to keep the memory of the Shoah alive and to pass it on so that mankind can learn from the past." Pavel starts breathing in great big gasps, and his voice becomes hoarse. "I stayed in Prague because it's been my family's home for more than six centuries. I've studied history and philosophy so that I could try to comprehend the incomprehensible. This period of history is so unique that we ought to hold on to what we know and try to find out even more. Israel is sacred to me, but I believe our place is among other peoples. If Israelis were to forsake Jewry, it would be a disaster. But if the Jews, if *we*, were to forsake the outside world, it would be equally devastating."

Pale, his back bent, Pavel returns to his seat. Some nod in agreement or even applaud. Sinai shakes his head in disapproval and stares straight ahead in aggrieved silence. John invites him to take his place at the table, but the rabbi prefers to stand next to his chair. All eyes are focused on him.

Sinai recites the centuries-old words of welcome to visitors to Jerusalem, "*Baruch Haba B'Shem Hashem*: Blessed is he who comes in the name of the Lord." He immediately apologizes for speaking in the German that we despise, but points out that translation creates barriers and that the purpose of our being here is to do away with barriers. About himself he says very little. He survived the death marches and was liberated together with some of the others in our group. He went to Prague, and then left a few months later for Palestine. He studied at a yeshiva and eventually became a chief rabbi. He's currently training other rabbis, and he hopes that the children of his children will one day choose the same path.

He tells his story as though it's a mere footnote. Then he straightens up and solemnly fixes each of us in turn with a piercing gaze. His voice gets louder, stronger. "The fact that there are still Jews living in the Diaspora after the Holocaust is an abomination to me. Remembering is not enough. The lesson to be learned from the Shoah is this: it is not just the Nazis who are cursed, but the entire German nation. Their best minds were put to work to figure out ways to kill us. But Germany wasn't the only one – other countries must also bear the guilt, because they watched from the sidelines. They turned a blind eye while the Germans tried to wipe us from the face of the earth. Jews are hated, and that hate is an incurable disease." Sinai casts his eyes upward and stretches his arms towards heaven: "Now that we have our own country, why wouldn't we want to live in it? He who makes peace in the heavens, may he make peace for us and all Israel! Amen."

The room is suddenly blanketed in silence. I feel annoyed and confused, as if I'd just been scolded for something I didn't do. Others look around in shock, seeking solace in the eyes of kindred spirits. The lesson the rabbi has learned from the past is not the one I or many of my friends have learned. His standpoint is still as far from mine as it was eight years ago in Jerusalem.

Ernst shifts restlessly in his chair. He puts the camera in his wife's lap and leaps to his feet the moment John starts his introduction. From his seat behind the table, he looks around in satisfaction and assures us he'll keep it short because he finds it hard to talk about the past. A sure sign, I fear, that a long monologue is about to follow.

He stumbles over his words. German expressions ring out like discordant notes in an otherwise English narrative. He thanks us again for holding the reunion and continues, his voice raw with emotion: "I don't know if there is such a thing as divine providence, but when I look at all of you here, so well educated and coming from all over the world, I thank God." He repeats his promise to keep it short. Hurriedly, like one possessed, he lets his memories take their course.

"I was born in Austria, near Vienna. I was *abtransportiert* [deported] to Theresienstadt along with my entire family. In May 1944 Rabbi Murmelstein, the Jewish Elder, told us our family was too big: '*Wir müssen euch leider nach Auschwitz schicken* [I'm afraid we're going to have to send you to Auschwitz].' I'd been badly burned in the shoe workshop, my mother had just had an operation, and my father couldn't walk anymore. And yet they put us on an *Arbeitstransport* [labor transport]." Staring straight ahead, he continues as if in a trance. "I dragged heavy soup kettles back and forth, just so I could lick them clean after everyone had been served. My mother used to sneak out of the barracks at night to take Father a piece of her bread. I saw the flames from the crematoriums but didn't know what they meant. I couldn't believe the stories I'd been told. When Mengele held his selection in July 1944, I tried to push my little brother through, but they didn't take him. My cousin Walter wanted to run over to his parents. He didn't understand what was about to happen to us all. I grabbed him and didn't let him go, even though he swore and struggled to get away. We were together until liberation. We helped keep each other alive. None of our relatives survived."

Ernst can contain his tears no longer. His voice choking, he goes on: "When the American bombers flew over Birkenau in September 1944 I begged God to let us die. No bombs fell on us, on the crematoriums, or on the train tracks. Six months ago I was in Auschwitz with a pair of twins who'd survived Mengele's experiments. For the first time I realized there were villages near the camp. Nobody did a thing to help us.

"I remember the uprising of the *Sonderkommando*. They were all killed. And I remember the death marches. They started evacuating everyone before the Russians reached Auschwitz. Walter and I were jammed into a freight car with two hundred other prisoners. No food, nothing to drink except, pardon me, urine. When we arrived in Buchenwald, only about twenty people in every car were still alive. During the night, as we waited outside in the freezing cold for the *Entlausing* [delousing], more people died."

Ernst's facial muscles relax slightly as he says, "Tony, our *Blockältester*, a Czechoslovakian Communist, did his best to protect us. The SS were looking for Jews in our barracks, and Tony snapped at them, '*In meinem Block gibt's keine Juden* [There aren't any Jews in my block].' They came back again the next day, and he hid us in the sewer pipes. We stayed there until the end, waiting for the Americans to liberate us."

Once again his eyes mist over. "There are more than ten men here, and one of us is even a rabbi. Let's say Kaddish for our families. Thank you."

Moved, we stare wordlessly in front of us. John, coolly cutting through the tension, asks Misha whether he'd prefer to speak before or after lunch. Yehuda, who has to go to work this afternoon, interrupts him. He expresses his thanks for the reunion and urges us to get together again two years from now, but then in Prague. John agrees, but Ernst wails, "Not in Prague, but in Auschwitz and Birkenau. That's where we should go. We owe it to the dead."

A murmur of protest ripples through the room. John's answer is meant to avoid the issue and still express our sentiments: "Let's just enjoy today's meeting." But Ernst is persistent: "There's nothing in Birkenau to remind people of what happened to our families. The memorial stone doesn't even contain the word 'Jews.' It's the same in Theresienstadt. Everything's gone, even the railroad tracks that transported us all to the East. When I came back from my trip, it made me sick to see how they'd covered up the Shoah."

Michael and John protest: we all heard Havel's attaché say yesterday that from now on things are going to be different! Why, the police museum in Theresienstadt is going to be transformed into a memorial center!

A flurry of wishes and opinions swirls through the room. Sinai, who hasn't joined the discussion, suddenly stands up and takes off his black hat. A velvet yarmulke of the kind favored by Orthodoxy is perched on his head. All conversation stops. We shove back our chairs to form a space facing east and look around for something to cover our heads with. Very few of the men have an actual yar-mulke – a black skullcap embroidered with silver thread or a knit one in bright colors. Most of us, including me, have to make do with handkerchiefs, caps, or cardboard hats. Our rustles are cut short by Sinai, who launches into the prayer for the dead. His first words are a signal for quiet. All around me are bowed heads, moving lips, and muttered words.

Thomas F., an assimilated Jew who's lived and worked in Germany for forty years, can't find an appropriate head covering. Not wanting to offend, he hesitantly puts his hand over his head. A moment later he reconsiders and casually scratches his head before lowering his arm again.

Like a magnet, Kaddish draws our emotions to the past. Our faces are even more deeply lined than before. Our eyes are filled with tears. The *Omein* brings us sharply back to the present. We pour out the door towards the light . . . towards lunch . . . towards normal life.

Stepping lightly, as though a weight has been lifted from our shoulders, we walk across a sunny park full of colorful flowers to the modern community center and dining hall. The kibbutzniks, including several elderly pioneers, are already seated at long tables, enjoying their meal. We pick up our trays and line up for the cafeteria-style lunch. Stainless-steel counters contain an ample array of unfamiliar but appetizing-looking food.

Ilana and Misha are in back of me. Misha puts his hand on my shoulder and asks in a whisper whether I have the same problem he does, namely a feeling of panic and fear when standing in lines. I hesitantly deny it, then suddenly remember how waiting lines used to fill me with rage.

*

Half an hour later we find ourselves back in the conference room, with Misha across from us. He surveys the listeners with a shy, boyish smile. His round glasses, stooped shoulders, thin face, and narrow English moustache peg him as a creative intellectual, but modestly he says nothing about his career as a prominent architect.

He pulls out a stack of papers and an old faded exercise book from his bag and aligns them neatly on the table. Toying nervously with a ballpoint pen, he says softly, "My diary is my link to the past. I wrote it a few weeks after liberation, in a sanatorium in the Tatra Mountains, on the advice of an army psychiatrist. Wolfie, who's now known as Sinai, arrived here with a briefcase full of memorabilia and a little diary identical to mine. We went to the store together to buy them. The paper has turned yellow and brittle, but the price, fifteen crowns, hasn't faded. Most of us were liberated from Gunskirchen forty-five years ago yesterday. That's how old our notebooks are. When Gerhard came to visit us in Boston, I took my diary out of a drawer and read it for the first time since I wrote it, because he brought up things I could no longer remember. Even today, I still feel like I'm reading about somebody else's life.

"The same sense of detachment occurs when I look at photographs. Yehuda is the exact opposite of me. His mind is like a camera. Maybe that's why he's such a wonderful painter. I don't have that ability. I often wonder if my memory is deceiving me. Can I really picture my parents, or am I remembering a photograph? Can my amnesia be cured by reading books on the subject and listening to our stories?

"My diary is my memory. Still, I vaguely recall a few

things. Why am I telling you this? Because I have two contradictory desires. I want to use the experiences and stories of others to fill in the blanks in my own past, and at the same time I'm afraid of being burdened by the knowledge. For a long time I tormented myself, wondering whether there was some point to recalling the horrors, or whether I should turn my back on the past. I finally concluded that we must bear witness so that the world won't forget. When Gerhard was in Boston, he took me with him to meet Elie Wiesel. We had a friendly chat with this sensitive, highly respected man. This visit reaffirmed my belief that our task is to pass on our knowledge.

"Some of us can't or won't accept this mission. They are not with us today – afraid of the confrontation, afraid of losing the emotional equilibrium they've worked so hard to achieve. In my diary I mention a friend I had in Birkenau. A handsome blond boy who was put to work, like me, as a *Läufer*, an errand boy. He lives in Boston, and he still remembers almost everything, though he rarely talks about it. He's afraid of opening up the past again, and he wants to protect himself and his family. I don't think we can blame him or condemn him.

"Within our group we have a wide range of opinions. Some of us think we should live in Israel, that only religion can save us. Some of us can't (or won't) accept the fact that God saw what was going on, and others deny his existence. I don't have enough discipline to search methodically through my past. I don't read about it, or write about it, but I admire those who do. Today I've realized that we have to pass our knowledge on to coming generations."

Misha isn't sure whether to stop or go on. We wait

quietly and expectantly, unwilling to let him go just yet. His gaze turns inward. His voice is hoarse. "The adults who went through the horror probably suffered more than we did. They were afraid for us as well as for themselves. Our childish minds could occasionally escape reality. We were helped by teachers like Freddy Hirsch. When he realized that we were doomed, he committed suicide. That was a disaster. But maybe some of us have been able to retain a little bit of that child's world?

"Already in Theresienstadt Freddy was able to keep many youngsters from going completely wild. I remember the frustration and envy I felt towards those who lived in Youth House L 417, because you had been forged into such a close-knit group. Some of you were fortunate enough to be part of that elite, the 'Harvard' of Theresienstadt. When I saw you here, those same childish feelings came over me again. The ties we formed in our youth are stronger than any we form in old age. I thank Yehuda and Gerhard for having made it possible for us to renew and strengthen these contacts after years of wandering."

He stands up while we clap, then remembers something and sits down again. He looks more relaxed, as if a weight has been lifted from his shoulders. "In the museum across the way I looked at a map showing the number of Jews deported from the occupied countries of Europe and the circuitous routes the Nazis used to drag them from one camp to another. I'd like to produce a similar map for us, to show how we wandered from country to country and from one continent to another after the war. I hope you'll all help."

Misha nods towards the listeners and returns to his place. Before he's even had time to take his seat, John begins reading more letters from "boys," without giving himself or us time for reflection.

The names aren't familiar to me. They weren't on my list, and I listen in surprise as everybody starts shouting out names of survivors they've either seen, or talked to, or heard about from others. For several minutes the room resembles a swap meet, with avid collectors trying to track down rare specimens. I have trouble making myself heard, but finally manage to ask if all those people were survivors of "our" group.

The excitement dies down. Reality prevails. It seems they've been talking about people who'd been in Theresienstadt's youth houses or had been transported from the Family Camp before the selection. I suddenly realize the reason for the outburst: our need to comfort ourselves amid the agonizing loneliness of survival.

Any semblance of order has now disappeared. Everyone starts talking at once about their various trials and tribulations. With no display of emotion except for an occasional break in their voices, people are dredging up gruesome memories of the death marches in the winter of '44–'45 or describing their liberation, which almost came too late.

Michael's quiet voice makes itself heard above the chaos. After his first measured words – "I was Mengele's errand boy in the infirmary" – the noise stops abruptly. "The hospital barracks was in the back of the camp, and Mengele came there twice a week. I ran all over the camp, doing his errands. He'd order me to fetch a pair of rubber gloves or a bottle of ammonia, or take a letter to his assistant, Fat Bertha, in the Gypsy Camp. Everything had to be done on the double. I never spoke to him, and all he ever did was snap out orders for little, insignificant things.

"There was a Jewish doctor he apparently respected. He addressed him as *Herr Kollege*. He'd been a famous professor of pediatrics in Germany. Eppstein was his name. Mengele had him perform operations without anesthetics. They were out of ether." Michael shakes his head as if to shake off the memories. "I can't talk about this with my sons. They don't want to hear a word, not a single word, about the camps. I've been looking into my genealogy. My ancestors were famous rabbis in Poland. Maybe that'll be of interest to them. Although with all those pogroms, who knows . . .? Anyway, that story isn't as humiliating as mine."

Michael's words upset me. I try to switch them off, to silence my own ghosts, but I'm having a hard time. One question has been haunting me for years. If ever there was a time and a place to ask it, this is it. "Why were we, and no one else, selected by Mengele and taken off to the Men's Camp, when everyone else in the Family Camp was doomed to die?"

There's a short silence, as if I've broken a taboo. I wait for an answer, feeling no need to offer my own theory. Eli mutters something about a witness who supposedly claimed during the Nuremberg trials that there was a shortage of errand boys in the other camps. Elimelech suggests that they kept us so we could be exchanged for German POWs.

Michael leans back in his chair and takes the floor again. "I've racked my brains wondering about that, but I still haven't come up with a satisfactory answer. The Germans rarely did anything spontaneously, without a plan or reason. After we were put in Block 13 of the Men's Camp, I established contact with a couple of men in the *Sonderkommando* in Block 11, because I spoke Polish. They helped me with food and clothes that they'd smuggled out of the gas chambers. One of them, a man named Gele, urged me to get out of Block 13 as quickly as possible and hide in a work unit somewhere else in the camp.

"Many of you also had protectors. They kind of adopted us. We were substitutes for their murdered children. At the end of the day, when they came back from working in the furnaces, they were broken, and they cried or stared vacantly into space.

"I never used to understand why Gele told me to leave Block 13. Now I think I know: he was afraid the Germans would use us as hostages to keep the men in the *Sonderkommando* in line. After the uprising in Crematorium IV, they were all killed, and we were once again fair game."

Our faces are pale. The nightmare has gone on into day. I feel like running out of the room, but I know it's pointless. I stand up and tell what I've found out.

Willy Bachmann, the *Lagerältester* of the Family Camp, was a German *Grünwinkel*. "Green triangles" were common criminals who'd been imprisoned for murders or other crimes. Willy was appointed as Camp Elder because he was a German and of "Aryan" blood. He was a conceited man, invariably dressed in riding outfits and boots pilfered from the suitcases and knapsacks of the imprisoned or the dead, but he ruled over the camp without being unduly bloodthirsty or sadistic. He seemed to get on well with the SS officers and was no more corrupt than most. It was rumored that he had a Jewish girlfriend. The same was said of Birkenau's commandant, Johan

Schwarzhuber. In July 1944, after the selections and transports, when the 7,000 remaining women, children, and old people were awaiting their destruction, the two Jewish mistresses begged their German boyfriends to spare the lives of some of the young boys. Schwarzhuber apparently heeded their pleas. He ordered us to appear for a selection, thereby coming in conflict with Mengele, who wanted to conduct the selection himself.

"Eighty-nine boys then crossed the border between life and death. We are all that remains."

Exhausted and trembling with emotion, I sit down. The air is thick with tension. I wait for somebody to comment or object. Silence. I've touched on forbidden territory.

Thomas, with his white hair and beard, is sitting by the window. His face has turned red, and he begins to breathe faster and heavier. Words come out of his mouth, hard and hoarse: "I was Willy's errand boy. He smuggled me over the main street of the camp, the *Lagerstrasse*, and into the Men's Camp so I didn't have to go through Mengele's selection. His girlfriend was my cousin. I don't want you talking about her."

A name is called from the back of the room. Thomas turns around, beside himself with rage. "That's right, she's still alive," he screams. "So now do you get it?"

I'm horrified. The tragic truth is even crueler than I suspected.

Thomas's revelation holds us in a spell that's broken only by John's stentorian tenor. Gratefully, I listen to his request for two minutes of silence in honor of our comrades who didn't come back. With a feeling of catharsis, we bid each other farewell. Sad but also relieved – friends who will always be each other's memento mori.

TO LIFE

My search has ended in a forest of questions. How did we survive, how could we go on living after the catastrophe? There are no adequate answers. Every answer generates new questions.

For a long time the ideas of Bruno Bettelheim, the psychoanalyst who was imprisoned in Dachau and Buchenwald in 1938 and 1939, dominated our thinking about "survival." According to Bettelheim, the extreme deprivation in the camps, the massive reign of terror by the SS and their helpers, the constant fears for one's life, the cruel abuse, the hunger, the back-breaking work, and the astronomical number of deaths depersonalized the prisoners, reduced them to an infantile state, and transformed them into unresisting creatures who either let themselves be led to the slaughter like sheep or, if they survived the first weeks of their internment, identified with their captors.

My own experience, plus the reading of personal testimonies, and the long conversations I've had with others who have shared my fate, have strengthened me in my conviction that this is an oversimplification. It also turns us into pathetic caricatures.

The idea of prisoners docilely surrendering to their oppressors without a single form of resistance or protest is a questionable generalization. Resistance in the camps, whether spontaneous or organized, was not what a romantic outsider imagines. Uprisings, armed revolts, or heroic battles against those in power were virtually impossible, which is why they occurred only sporadically. Resistance and opposition took other forms. There were many who neither accepted the brutality nor forgot who they were. Maneuvering between Scylla and Charybdis, they tried to keep the horror from sinking in, formed small groups that provided solidarity, committed minute acts of sabotage, and were alert to the signs of danger. Far from alleviating the so-called survivor guilt among former prisoners, a romanticized notion of resistance only makes it worse.

Anyone who wants to understand what it was like to be in the concentration camps will have to ask why the Nazis set them up in the first place. After the Wannsee Conference on January 20, 1942, it was no longer possible to have any illusions about their ultimate aim: the annihilation of all Jewish prisoners and anyone else the authorities considered to be inferior and/or dangerous to the state. One thing is clear: had the Allies taken much longer in 1945 to reach the camps, there would have been almost no one left to liberate.

Soon after the Nazis rose to power in 1933, they ordered the construction of several concentration camps. In the beginning these fell under the jurisdiction of Hitler's Stormtroopers, the SA. The Columbia-Haus in Berlin, for example, was directly under Göring's control. Communists, Socialists, disenchanted supporters, purged

Nazis, and Jews were all locked away from the world, tortured, and executed there. Many others wound up in Dachau, Buchenwald, Sachsenhausen-Oranienburg, and Flossenburg, concentration camps built after 1933. The extermination camps – Treblinka, Sobibor, and Auschwitz – came into being only in 1939 and 1940.

The construction of every concentration camp cost the lives of thousands of prisoners. On the orders of the Head Office for Reich Security, the RSHA, the prisoners were shipped to a barren stretch of land where they were forced to build their own dungeons out of virtually nothing. There were no shelters, no sanitary facilities, and almost no food. The *univers concentrationnaire*, to use David Rousset's expression, sprang out of the ground like a poisonous mushroom.

One of the most important functions of these places of doom was to act as a deterrent. Their mere existence was enough to strike terror into the heart of anyone who hadn't sold his soul to the Nazis. Which is not to say that the entire population knew about the atrocities from the start. Prior to 1939, prisoners were occasionally released and allowed to go home. But they didn't dare discuss the hell they'd been in – the Gestapo kept them under constant surveillance. Even those who had emigrated or been exiled kept their lips sealed, for fear of the German secret service. The few who did speak out found that their stories were either nipped in the bud or chalked up to fantasy. After all, until the war broke out Germany was our friend. A friendship that many refugees, turned back at the border, paid for with their lives.

Another function of the camps was to serve as a training ground for amorality. *Polizie-SS-Führer* Theodor

Eicke split his Death Head Regiment off from the SS and put his men to work as camp guards. The idea was to turn them into a crack unit of hardened individuals with no scruples whatsoever (assuming they had any in the first place). They were recruited from the same groups as the Stormtroopers: frustrated tradespeople, unemployed laborers, craftsmen, fanatical Wehrmacht soldiers, etc. For the officer corps: jobless white-collar workers, teachers, police and army officers with no chance of promotion, Nazi supporters whose consciences didn't balk at political murder.

Under Eicke's direction, these SS men were trained to hate and kill indiscriminately. They looked on prisoners as vermin, or less than vermin, who deserved to be exploited and exterminated. They might make an exception for an occasional German criminal. Common criminals in Germany were sent to the camps for "re-education," though they too were rarely released. They were frequently put to work as outright accomplices of the SS. As kapos, *Blockältesten*, and *Lagerältesten*, they formed a mafia-like network of graft and corruption. Political prisoners were almost never appointed to these jobs. Towards the end of the war, Buchenwald was an exception to this rule. The criminals had made such a mess of things that the SS was obliged to replace them with political prisoners. In so doing, many a life was saved.

Another function of the camps, to work people to death, typifies the absurdity of the system. The often-heard claim that the camps made use of slave labor is based on a fallacy. In the past, slaves represented capital to their owners. Since they had to be strong enough to work, their basic needs were taken care of. In the concentration-camp universe, work was a means of destruction. Prisoners who were exhausted were relegated to the scrap heap. Such wastage of human lives is unparalleled in history.

In the last year of the war, Oswald Pohl of the Head Office for Administration and Economy, the WVHA, protested against this misuse of labor. Not out of a gush of humanity, mind you, but because the slaves were needed for the war industry.

Until the outbreak of the war, the camps also functioned as a holding pen for hostages. Jews in particular were used by the Nazis to blackmail other countries, so that they could carry out their war plans with impunity. After the Germans invaded Poland and war was declared, the mass slaughter of Baltic Jews began almost immediately. At the same time, mass executions took place in Buchenwald.

To an outsider it must seem incredible that a relatively small number of SS men was able to keep 100,000 prisoners under control and even, in the latter years of the war, herd millions to their deaths. Resistance, sabotage, and escape did occur, though infrequently. Not because the prisoners were passive or cowardly or had lost the will to live. Under such circumstances labels like these are misleading. Nor were the gruesome reprisals the only reason the SS was able to maintain its reign of terror. After all, we lived with a constant threat of death. The question wasn't whether we would die, but how.

The SS's strategy for prisoner control was one that had been tried and tested throughout the ages – Machiavelli was no stranger to the technique. It consisted of deliberately playing one victim against another and consistently pursuing a divide-and-rule policy. The camps were set up to capitalize on differences in nationality, religion, gender, age, disposition, and status. Moreover, the SS had an unerring instinct for evil: they knew exactly how to find kindred spirits who were more than willing to relieve them of their task.

We usually associate the term "mass extermination" with the Zyklon-B gas used in Auschwitz, Treblinka, and Sobibor. However, it wasn't that simple: Bergen-Belsen didn't have a gas chamber, and yet tens of thousands died of starvation, neglect, and disease. Mauthausen was equipped with a gas chamber only towards the end of the war; before then prisoners were shot, bludgeoned to death, or crushed by stones in the quarries. There are more examples, too many and too awful to enumerate. Suffice it to say that many roads led to the final destination. Each camp had its favorite route, but they all took us down the same paths and watched us disappear.

Questions keep coming back and buzzing around my head like hornets. How could people survive those hells? How could they keep going for months and even years? How could they go on living after the smoking chimneys of Birkenau?

Very few of us who made it to the end of the war were able to grasp the miracle of liberation. When we returned to the countries we came from, we were seldom welcomed with open arms. People didn't want to be reminded of their troubles or confronted with someone else's. We found it hard to express ourselves, so we cooperated in the silence. As soon as our ravaged bodies were well enough, we went to work.

Survival was a puzzle that we tried to solve with guilt: why us and not them? Were we tougher, luckier, better, worse? I don't have an answer to these questions. Nor does anyone else.

Of course we hazard guesses as to why our chances of survival were a fraction better than those of the older prisoners who saw their families go up in smoke. While most of us lost our parents the same way, it's possible that the reverse – the loss of one's spouse and children – leaves deeper wounds in an adult. Besides, we were young and healthy. Most of us had had doting parents and hadn't suffered poverty. Over the years we'd learned to be alert to danger and intuitively knew where help could be expected.

By the time liberation came, we were human wrecks. Seventy-five percent of the boys in our group died in the last year of the war.

"We're living on borrowed time," we all say. It's our way of referring to the puzzle to which we have no answer.

With the consummate irony of a longtime victim of persecution, a Polish Jew said to me soon after liberation, "Anyone who comes out of the camps halfway normal must be out of his mind." I was reminded of this when Honza S. and his wife came to visit me a few weeks after I got back from Canada. He brought along the questionnaire I'd sent him two years earlier.

I didn't recognize him after all this time, though his slightly protruding eyes seemed vaguely familiar. He and Yvette were a good-looking couple. He walked with a very self-assured bearing. You could see by his figure that he was fit and by his tan that he got plenty of Brazil's sunshine. They had come directly from São Paulo.

His friends Robin in Toronto and Misha in Boston had already told me what his nickname was in 1945. He didn't know it at the time, but they'd called him "Gorilla." Only later, when he'd recovered, did the psychologist at the Hörsching air force base explain why.

Honza (who re-named himself Ian when he moved to another continent) was liberated by American troops along with some of the other "boys" from a camp near Gunskirchen. He was sent to a hospital to recuperate from typhoid fever and other diseases he'd contracted in the camps. Since he and his friends had approximately the same illnesses, they found themselves in the same ward. One day he suddenly went berserk and starting smashing up the furniture. He managed to evade the nurses by swinging from the beams like a gorilla and hiding in the attic, in the cellar, and behind cupboards. He no longer recognized anyone, and he shrieked in panic until he was finally carried off in a straitjacket.

Now Honza is seated across from me in my study, with the questionnaire on his knees. He barely looks at it – he's familiar with its contents. As if he wants to remove any doubts I might have about his sanity, he refers immediately to his breakdown and the months of total amnesia that followed. He talks about it without inhibition, even with a certain amount of self-ridicule.

His camp years are very similar to those of Robin and his brother Martin. His prewar existence differed only slightly. His father wasn't an intellectual. His mother was very artistic, and, as an only child, he was the focal point of their parental solicitude.

In Theresienstadt he was assigned to L 417, the youth house whose famous teachers tried to instill their charges with more than mere learning. Sentries were posted to signal the approach of guards, who'd been ordered to put a halt to any sign of educational activity. Honza's father spent his evenings, after a long day at work, writing out lessons and slipping them to his son to make sure he wouldn't be illiterate. "I've never forgotten some of them. A few days before Passover, he filled a large sheet of paper with drawings of pharaohs and pyramids, and he wrote down their names: Ramses, Tutankhamen, Cheops, Gizeh."

I'd arrived in Birkenau on the same transport, and we'd gone through the same selection. Honza, standing next to the tall and athletic Robin and Martin, failed to pass the inspection. Robin advised him to go back in line and stand beside someone smaller. "I had number A-1832, the other kid had number A-1831. We'd ridden to Auschwitz in the same boxcar. We stood there in front of Mengele, and he was rejected while I made it through."

Ian's eyes focus on some invisible point in the distance, as if he can see the past there. He muses out loud, hardly aware of his listener: "Mengele was a handsome man, and I had the idiotic idea that he'd spare us. I was incredibly superstitious then, and I thought God would help me. Sometimes I'd bore my eyes into the back of an SS man. I thought I could kill him with a look, by sheer force of will. The next day I'd see him at roll call and feel like God had betrayed me. After that, whenever I saw people praying,

I'd be furious. Why didn't they revolt? Why didn't they fight back?"

His agitation over, he addresses his comments to me again. Several anecdotes follow. "We were rich once, there in the Men's Camp. Well, for a few days anyway. Robin and I had pinched a bag of salt. About that time there was a delivery problem, and the kitchens were having to cook without salt. We traded our salt for shoes, shirts, a blanket. I even had a knife. All of a sudden there was salt in the food again, and our supply became worthless overnight."

His story begins to lose all sense of chronology. He tells me about his anxiety dreams, then and now, about the nightmares that torment him, and about his guardian angel, a Communist named Bully who saved his life by letting him hide among the political prisoners. I ask whether he ever thought about life beyond the barbed-wire fences, about normal life with plenty of food, heat, music, and beautiful books. He grins. "The only thing I thought about in camp was how to survive. Nothing else. How and where I could steal food and clothes, what I had to do to avoid heavy or dangerous work, how I could 'organize' a spoon, a soup bowl, a knife, a piece of string to hold up my pants, a pair of shoes that fit.

"We had a kind of commune, Robin, Martin, Paul, and I. We shared everything. Except that Paul cheated. We kicked him out, but he managed okay on his own. I was very precise, and I planned our transactions and pilfering raids very carefully. A French professor, a Maquisard we called *le maître*, taught me how to get by. Or as he put it, *se débrouiller*.

"After the war a family in Prague took me in. They were

nice to me, but they had marital problems. She tried to commit suicide a couple of times and finally wound up in an asylum. I went to see her often, but I was always afraid they wouldn't let me out. He was a Communist bigwig and was hardly ever home."

His story makes me ache with sadness. I see the dark streets of Prague and a lonely and confused fourteen-year-old boy left to fend for himself, and I project my own return to Holland on the screen of my memory.

The anger in Ian's voice is evident as he recalls the incident that made him decide to leave the country. "It happened my first day of high school. This kid was standing in the doorway to the classroom, blocking my way. He said to me with a nasty grin, 'No Jews allowed.' I hit him so hard I knocked a couple of teeth out, and that was the end of my education."

He continues, almost cheerfully, "I was sent to an uncle of mine in London. He shipped me off to boarding school so I wouldn't be underfoot. After a couple of months I ran away and wound up in a hostel for camp children in Scotland. They put me in a kibbutz-like farm camp that prepared you for life in Israel. I became more Jewish than I'd ever been before. I don't mean religious or anything, but more aware of my identity. I was somebody again. They trained me to be a car mechanic and an electrician. I wanted to join the Israeli army, but instead I ended up in South America. Just as I was about to leave for Israel, a relative invited me to come to Rio de Janeiro.

"I stayed on in a continent that offered endless opportunities. I earned good money and finally realized that there's more to life than I'd thought. Getting by, *se débrouiller*, isn't enough. Like my friend Robin, I believe that art is not just a frill but an essential ingredient to life."

For a moment it's quiet. Then he gives me a hard look. "As for that business in the doorway at school," he says, "I still do it. I don't let anyone scoff at my Jewishness."

We join our wives in the living room. The two women, radiating concern from every pore, search our faces as if we're mineworkers emerging from a cave-in. We have indeed been delving into the dark tunnels of our past. But we haven't been crushed by the rubble. Ian least of all. It occurs to me that he's integrated the black years of his youth better than many of us.

We sit down and chat as though we're at a casual tea party. Everything is so normal, so comfy. We hover above the abyss and pretend it's not there.

Yvette, whose parents were deported to the East from Drancy and never seen again, is wearing a thin gold chain around her neck with the Hebrew *chai* sign: חי, a reminder of the Talmudic respect for life. She notices my glance, touches the necklace, and says with a smile, "We take it very much to heart."

1982–1990

A WORD OF THANKS

Several institutes gave me access to their trial records and eyewitness reports. I'm grateful to their staffs for their interest, understanding, and hospitality. In particular I wish to thank the Rijksinstituut voor Oorlogsdocumentatie in Amsterdam, the archives of Yad Vashem in Jerusalem, the Wiener Library in London, the Centre Documentation Juive Contemporaire in Paris, and the Center for Holocaust Studies in Brooklyn. The Stichting Fonds voor de Letteren, the Etty Hillesum Stichting, and the Februari 1941 Fonds made it financially possible for me to visit archives and interview my fellow survivors.

The friendliness and cordiality I encountered in many countries during my conversations with my fellow "boys" helped lessen the burden and pain of this subject. I now have a strong tie with many of them.

Tilly Hermans, my editor at Meulenhoff, was unfailingly creative, critical, and full of interest. Her encouraging words were always accompanied by sympathy and understanding.

Without my wife's dedication and listening head and heart, this book could never have been written.